What A World 1

Amazing Stories from Around the Globe

Milada Broukal

What a World 1: Amazing Stories from Around the Globe

Pearson Education, 10 Bank Street, White Plains, NY 10606

Vice president, multimedia and skills: Sherry Preiss
Senior acquisitions editor: Laura Le Dréan
Development editor: Andrea Bryant
Production editor: Andréa C. Basora
Vice president of domestic marketing: Kate McLoughlin
Vice president of international marketing: Bruno Paul
Senior manufacturing buyer: Nancy Flaggman
Photo research: Dana Klinek
Cover and text design: Elizabeth Carlson
Text composition: Color Associates
Text font: 12/15 New Aster
Photo credits: **Page 1,** AP/Wide World Photos. **Page 8,** © Corbis/Phil
Schermeister. **Page 13,** © Stone/Getty Images. **Page 19,** AP/Wide World
Photos. **Page 25,** © Corbis/Charles & Josette Lenars. **Page 31,** © Robin
Sachs/PhotoEdit. **Page 37,** AP/Wide World Photos. **Page 43,** © Corbis/
Dallas and John Heaton. **Page 49,** © Corbis/Janet Wishnetsky. **Page 55,**
© Jeff Greenberg/ PhotoEdit. **Page 65,** © Corbis/Underwood & Underwood.
Page 71, © Corbis/ Dave G. Houser. **Page 77,** © Corbis/Paul A. Souders.
Page 83, © Corbis/ Lindsay Hebberd. **Page 89,** © Mark Richards/PhotoEdit.
Page 95, © Corbis/ Owen Franken. **Page 101,** AP/Wide World Photos.
Page 107, © Corbis/ Patrick Ward. **Page 113,** © Corbis/Paul Seheult; Eye
Ubiquitous. **Page 119,** © Corbis/Araldo de Luca.

Library of Congress Cataloging-in-Publication Data
Broukal, Milada.
    What a world!:amazing stories from around the globe. bk 1/Milada Broukal.
        p. cm.
    ISBN 0-13-048462-8 (alk. paper)
      1. English language—Textbooks for foreign speakers. 2. Readers. I. Title

PE1128.B7165 2004
428.6'4—dc22

                                                    2003060306

ISBN: 0-13-048462-8
ISBN: 0-13-184925-5 (book with audio CD)

Printed in the United States of America
1 2 3 4 5 6 7 8 9 10–VHJ–08 07 06 05 04

CONTENTS

INTRODUCTION

What A World: Amazing Stories from Around the Globe is a beginning reader. It is the first in a two-book series of readings for students of English as a second or foreign language. Twenty topics have been selected for this book. Each topic is about a different person, place, or custom. The topics span history and the globe, from J.K. Rowling, to life in Antarctica, to the history of body decoration.

Every unit begins with a question and answers that question. Each unit contains:

- A prereading activity
- A reading passage (300–400 words)
- Topic-related vocabulary work
- Comprehension exercises, including pair work
- Discussion questions
- A writing activity
- A spelling and punctuation activity

BEFORE YOU READ opens with a picture of the person, place, or custom featured in the unit. Prereading questions follow. Their purpose is to motivate students to read, encourage predictions about the content of the reading, and involve the students' own experiences when possible. Vocabulary can be presented as the need arises.

The **READING** passage should be first done individually by skimming for the general content. The teacher may wish to explain the bolded vocabulary words at this point. The students should then do a second, closer reading. Further reading(s) can be done aloud. If you have the Student Book with the accompanying Audio CD, you can use it in the classroom or have the students listen at home.

The two **VOCABULARY** exercises focus on the bolded words in the reading. *Meaning*, a definition exercise, encourages students to work out the meanings from the context. Within this group are *Words that Go Together*—collocations or groups of words which are easier to learn together the way they are used in the language. The second exercise, *Use*, reinforces the vocabulary further by making students use the words in a meaningful, yet possibly different, context. This section can be done during or after the reading phase, or both.

There are several **COMPREHENSION** exercises. Each unit contains *Understanding the Reading* and *Remembering Details*. These are followed by either *Understanding the Sequence* or *Sentence Completion*. All confirm the content of the text either in general or in detail. These exercises for developing reading skills can be done individually, in pairs, in small groups, or as a class. It is preferable to do these exercises in conjunction with the text, since they are not meant to test memory. The comprehension exercises end with *Tell the Story* or *Dictation* which are speaking activities.

DISCUSSION questions encourage students to bring their own ideas and imagination to the related topics in each reading. They can also provide insights into cultural similarities and differences.

WRITING provides the stimulus for students to write simple sentences about the reading. Teachers should use their own discretion when deciding whether or not to correct the writing exercises.

SPELLING AND PUNCTUATION provides basic rules and accompanying activities for spelling or punctuation, using examples from the readings. An index listing the spelling and punctuation activities can be found on page 132.

SELF-TESTS after Unit 10 and Unit 20 review sentence structure, vocabulary, and spelling and punctuation in a multiple-choice format.

There are three **APPENDICES**: a Word List, organized by unit; a Map of the World; and an Index to the Spelling and Punctuation Activities.

If you would like the Answer Key for *What A World 1,* please contact Pearson Longman.
Customers in the United States: ESLSampling@pearsoned.com
Customers outside the United States: elt@pearsoned.com

UNIT 1

Who Is
J.K. Rowling?

BEFORE YOU READ

Answer these questions.

1. What do you know about *Harry Potter*?
2. Is *Harry Potter* a real person?
3. How many *Harry Potter* books are there?

Who Is J.K. Rowling?

1 J.K. Rowling is the **author** of the *Harry Potter* books. J.K.'s name is Joanne Kathleen. She was born in 1965 in a small town near Bristol, England. Joanne lived with her parents and her sister. The Rowling family was not rich. Joanne did not go to **special** schools. She was a **quiet** child. She loved to read and write stories. Joanne went to Exeter University, and she finished in 1987. She worked in different offices. In her **free time**, she wrote more stories.

2 In 1990, Joanne's mother died. Joanne was sad, and she wanted to leave England. She saw a job in the newspaper for an English teacher. The job was in Portugal. She had an **interview**, and she got the job. In Portugal, Joanne married a Portuguese man. The next year, Joanne had a daughter, but she was not happy in her marriage. She left Portugal with her daughter and went to live in Edinburgh, Scotland, near her sister.

3 Life was very difficult for Joanne. She **took care of** her daughter. She was **alone**, and nobody helped her. She had no money and no job. She lived in a small apartment and began to write stories again. Joanne first thought about the *Harry Potter* story many years ago on a train. Joanne liked to go to a coffee shop to write. She sat there for many hours. She drank coffee and wrote. Her daughter slept beside her.

4 After five years, Joanne finished writing the first *Harry Potter* book. She sent it to many book publishers. They all said that they didn't like it. Finally, a publisher liked it, but the publisher said, "This is a children's book. **Adults** won't read it. You won't **make** a lot of **money**." In 1997, *Harry Potter and the Sorcerer's Stone* was in the bookstores. J.K. Rowling was very happy. Her dream to publish her book **came true**. The book was famous **all over the world**.

5 Now *Harry Potter* is in forty-two languages. The publisher was wrong about one thing: Everyone loves *Harry Potter*—children and adults. Over 100 million books were sold in 1999. Then two *Harry Potter* books became movies. J.K. Rowling wrote three more *Harry Potter* books after that. People all over the world want more *Harry Potter*. And what is J.K. Rowling doing now? She is writing another book!

VOCABULARY

MEANING

Write the correct words in the blanks.

interview	quiet	adults
author	special	alone

1. J.K. Rowling is an _____. She writes books.
2. Joanne was not a noisy child. She was _____.
3. Joanne went to regular, ordinary schools. She did not go to _____ schools.
4. Children like *Harry Potter*. _____ like *Harry Potter*, too. People of all ages like *Harry Potter*.
5. Joanne lived _____. She did not live with another person.
6. Joanne had a meeting about a new job. She had an _____.

WORDS THAT GO TOGETHER

Write the correct words in the blanks.

free time	came true	took care of
make money	all over the world	

1. Joanne wrote when she didn't work. She wrote stories in her _____.
2. Joanne watched and helped her daughter. She _____ her.
3. Joanne writes books, and the book publisher pays her. She will _____.
4. *Harry Potter* is famous in every country. It is famous _____.
5. Good things happened to Joanne. All of her dreams _____.

USE

Work with a partner to answer the questions. Use complete sentences.

1. Who is the *author* of this book?
2. What do you do when you are *alone*?
3. Who is a *quiet* student in your class?
4. What do you do in your *free time*?
5. What fast food is famous *all over the world*?
6. What questions do people ask at an *interview*?

COMPREHENSION

UNDERSTANDING THE READING

Circle the letter of the correct answer.

1. Joanne was _____.
   a. not from a rich family   b. from a big family   c. a bad child

2. Joanne _____ and went to Portugal.
   a. got a job   b. got married   c. wrote her book

3. *Harry Potter* is a book for _____.
   a. children   b. adults   c. children and adults

REMEMBERING DETAILS

Circle *T* if the sentence is true. Circle *F* if the sentence is false.

1. Joanne was an English teacher in Portugal.	T	F
2. Joanne married an English man in Portugal.	T	F
3. Joanne left her daughter in Portugal.	T	F
4. Joanne finished writing the first *Harry Potter* book after five years.	T	F
5. Every publisher liked her book.	T	F
6. *Harry Potter* is in forty-two languages.	T	F

UNDERSTANDING THE SEQUENCE

Which happened first? Write *1* on the line. Which happened second? Write *2* on the line.

1. _____ Joanne became an English teacher.

   _____ Joanne worked in different offices.

2. _____ Joanne thought about *Harry Potter* on the train.

   _____ Joanne wrote about *Harry Potter* in the coffee shop.

3. _____ Joanne finished *Harry Potter*.

   _____ Joanne sent *Harry Potter* to publishers.

4. _____ Two *Harry Potter* books became movies.

   _____ *Harry Potter* was in the bookstores.

TELL THE STORY

Work with a partner. Tell the story of J.K. Rowling to your partner. Use your own words. Your partner asks you questions about the story. Then your partner tells you the story and you ask questions.

DISCUSSION

Discuss the answers to these questions with your classmates.

1. Why is *Harry Potter* so popular?
2. The *Harry Potter* story is not real. Do you like to read stories that are real or not real? Why?
3. Adults and children like *Harry Potter*. What are other books or movies that adults and children like?

WRITING

Complete the sentences about J.K. Rowling.

Example: J.K. Rowling is *an author.* _____

1. J.K. Rowling wrote _____
2. Joanne is from _____
3. Joanne worked _____
4. Joanne married _____
5. *Harry Potter* is _____

SPELLING AND PUNCTUATION

 CAPITAL LETTERS: NAMES, PLACES, NATIONALITIES, AND LANGUAGES

We use a capital letter for:

People's names and initials

*Joanne **R**owling and **J.K. R**owling are the same person.*

Names of cities, states, countries, and continents

London   **Florida**   **Portugal**   **Africa**

Nationalities and languages

***A**mericans loved her book.*

*You can read her book in **S**panish, **F**rench, or **G**erman.*

A. Underline the words that need capital letters. The first one is done for you.

1. The name of the boy is <u>harry</u> potter.
2. Joanne rowling lived in edinburgh.
3. You can read *harry potter* in spanish.
4. She didn't go to spain, but she went to portugal.
5. She married a portuguese man.
6. She lived near bristol in england.
7. J.k. rowling went to the united states.
8. She loves the stories of e. nesbit and c.s. lewis.

B. Answer the questions. Use correct capital letters.

1. What is your father's full name? _____

2. Who is your favorite singer? _____

3. What nationality is he or she? _____

4. Who is your favorite actor or actress? _____

5. Where does he or she live? _____

UNIT 2

What Are Some Special Rules for Chinese New Year?

BEFORE YOU READ

Answer these questions.

1. What do you know about Chinese New Year?
2. When do you celebrate New Year's Day in your country?
3. How do you celebrate New Year's Day?

What Are Some Special Rules for Chinese New Year?

1   Chinese New Year is a special holiday. It starts on the first new moon of the Chinese **calendar** between January 21 and February 19. The New Year **celebration** ends fifteen days later on the day of the full moon. Chinese New Year is a very old celebration. The Chinese do something different on each day. People believe many old **superstitions** about this holiday. There are special rules about how people clean and what people **look like**. There are also rules about how people **act**.

2   The Chinese believe that it is very important to have a clean house on New Year's Day. They clean the house before New Year's Day. Then they **put away** everything they use to clean. The Chinese don't **sweep** the floor on New Year's Day. They think they will sweep away **good luck**. After New Year's Day, they sweep again. First they sweep the dirt from the door to the middle of the room. Then they sweep the dirt from the middle of the room to the corners of the room. They leave the dirt there for five days. On the fifth day, they sweep the dirt to the back door. The Chinese believe that it is bad luck to sweep the dirt to the front door.

3   The way people look on New Year's Day is also important. The Chinese do not wash their hair on New Year's Day. They believe they will wash away good luck. People also like to wear red clothes on New Year's Day. Red is a **bright**, happy color. It will bring good luck for the future.

4   The Chinese also have superstitions about how people act on New Year's Day. Older people give children and unmarried friends little red envelopes with money inside. The money is for good luck. People do not say bad or unlucky words. They do not say the word *four* because it sounds like the word for death. The Chinese never talk about death on New Year's Day. They also do not talk about the past year. They talk about the new year and new beginnings.

5   Today, some Chinese believe in these rules and some do not. But many people **practice** the rules. They are special **traditions**. The rules are part of Chinese **culture** and history.

VOCABULARY

MEANING

Write the correct words in the blanks.

calendar	superstitions	act	sweep	practice
celebration	bright	culture	traditions	

1. The Chinese New Year is a _____. It is a happy time that everyone enjoys.

2. The Chinese have some old _____. They believe that some things are good luck and some things are bad luck.

3. Do you know about Chinese _____? Their beliefs and way of life are interesting.

4. Before New Year's Day, the Chinese clean the floor. They use a broom to _____ it.

5. The Chinese believe in special rules for the New Year. They _____ the rules every year.

6. Red is a _____ color. It is strong and easy to see.

7. The Chinese _____ shows the days, months, and holidays in the year.

8. The Chinese do these things every year for many years. These things are _____ for them.

9. How do people _____ for Chinese New Year? What do they do and say?

WORDS THAT GO TOGETHER

Write the correct words in the blanks.

good luck	look like	put away

1. Is he wearing special clothes for New Year's Day? What does he _____?

2. The Chinese want _____. They want happy things to happen.

3. They took out the broom to clean. Now they are finished. So they _____ the broom.

USE

Work with a partner to answer the questions. Use complete sentences.

1. What is your favorite *celebration*?
2. What *superstitions* do you believe in?
3. What do you do for *good luck*?
4. What *bright* color do you like?
5. What special New Year's *tradition* do you have?
6. What do you *put away* at night?
7. How do you *act* on holidays?

COMPREHENSION

UNDERSTANDING THE READING

Circle the letter of the correct answer.

1. The Chinese New Year _____.
   a. starts on the full moon
   b. starts on the new moon
   c. ends on the new moon

2. The Chinese clean their houses _____.
   a. on New Year's Day
   b. before New Year's Day
   c. every day during the New Year celebration

3. The Chinese _____ for good luck on New Year's Day.
   a. wear new clothes
   b. give money to young people
   c. talk about the past year

REMEMBERING DETAILS

Reread the passage and answer the questions.

1. How many days is the Chinese New Year celebration?
2. Why don't the Chinese sweep on New Year's Day?
3. Why don't the Chinese wash their hair on New Year's Day?
4. What color do the Chinese wear on New Year's Day?
5. What do older people give children?
6. What word sounds like the word for *death*?

SENTENCE COMPLETION

Match the words in Column A and Column B to make sentences.

A	B
____ 1. The Chinese New Year is	a. their houses before New Year's Day.
____ 2. The Chinese clean	b. red clothes on New Year's Day.
____ 3. The Chinese don't say	c. a very old celebration.
____ 4. The Chinese New Year ends	d. bad words on New Year's Day.
____ 5. The Chinese don't wash	e. after fifteen days.
____ 6. The Chinese wear	f. their hair on New Year's Day.

DICTATION

Work with a partner. Read three sentences from the exercise above. Your partner listens and writes the sentences. Then your partner reads three sentences and you write them.

DISCUSSION

Discuss the answers to these questions with your classmates.

1. Do people in your country do special things for the New Year?
2. Is the New Year a happy time or a sad time? Why?
3. On New Year's Day in the United States, people talk about making changes. Some people say they are going to eat healthy food or get a new job. What do you want to do next year?

WRITING

Complete the sentences about your New Year's Day.

Example: New Year's Day is _on January 1 in my country._____

1. On New Year's Day, I wear _____
2. On New Year's Day, we eat _____
3. On New Year's Day, people don't _____
4. On New Year's Day, I like to _____
5. On New Year's Day, I don't like to _____

SPELLING AND PUNCTUATION

 CAPITAL LETTERS: DAYS, MONTHS, AND HOLIDAYS

We use a capital letter for:

Names of days
Monday   Friday   Sunday

Names of months
March   July   December

Names of holidays
New Year's Day   Thanksgiving   Christmas

We do <u>not</u> use a capital letter for the names of the seasons.
summer   winter   spring   autumn (fall)

A. Underline the words that need capital letters. Remember the capital letter rules from Unit 1.

1. Chinese new year comes between january 21 and february 19.
2. On new year's eve, chinese families get together to eat a big meal.
3. In the united states and europe, new year's eve is on december 31.
4. In south america, new year's day is in the summer.
5. The persians celebrate new year's day in the spring.
6. In canada, thanksgiving is in october.
7. Americans celebrate thanksgiving on the last thursday in november.
8. People in the united states celebrate independence on july 4.

B. Answer the questions. Use correct capital letters.

1. What is your favorite holiday? _____
2. In what month is your favorite holiday? _____
3. On what day of the week is this holiday this year? _____

UNIT 3

Where Is Buckingham Palace?

BEFORE YOU READ

Answer these questions.

1. Why is Buckingham Palace famous?
2. How many rooms does the palace have?
3. Is Buckingham Palace a home or an office?

Where Is Buckingham Palace?

1 Buckingham Palace is in London, England. Buckingham Palace was built around 1705. It is famous because Queen Elizabeth of England lives there. She became queen in 1952.

2 Buckingham Palace is a big and beautiful building. A **flag** flies at the palace. It flies **on top of** the palace when the queen is there. Queen Elizabeth and her family live on the second **floor** of the palace. The queen also has her office at the palace. Presidents, kings, and **politicians** meet with her. Queen Elizabeth often asks important people to eat dinner at the palace. She also has three **garden** parties in the summer. She invites 9,000 people to each party! **A lot of** people meet the queen.

3 Buckingham Palace is like a small town. It has a police station, a hospital, two post offices, a movie theater, a swimming pool, two sports clubs, a garden, and a lake. The palace has about 600 rooms. About 400 people work there. Two people have very unusual jobs. They take care of the clocks. There are 300 clocks in Buckingham Palace!

4 Queen Elizabeth's day starts at 7:00 in the morning. Seven people take care of her. One person **prepares** her bath, and another person prepares her clothes. Another person takes care of her dogs. The queen loves dogs. Right now, she has eight dogs. Every day, a man brings food for the dogs to Queen Elizabeth's room. The queen puts the food in the **bowls** with a silver spoon.

5 At 8:30 every morning, the queen has breakfast with her husband, Prince Philip. They drink a special coffee with hot milk. During breakfast, a musician plays Scottish music outside. Then Queen Elizabeth works in her office **the rest of** the morning. After lunch, she visits hospitals, schools, or new buildings.

6 It is very interesting to eat dinner at Buckingham Palace. You have to **follow rules**. Queen Elizabeth starts to eat first, and then everybody eats. When the queen finishes eating, everybody finishes eating. You can't leave the table during dinner. The queen never accepts a telephone call during dinner, even in an **emergency**.

7 People visit the rooms in Buckingham Palace in August and September. There are wonderful things to see, like paintings and statues. Don't forget that Queen Elizabeth is one of the richest people in the world.

VOCABULARY

MEANING

Write the correct words in the blanks.

politicians	flag	bowls	prepares
garden	emergency	floor	

1. Buckingham Palace has a place with flowers and plants. It has a

   _____.

2. The queen doesn't get her clothes ready. A person _____ the queen's clothes for her.

3. The prime minister and the president are important _____. They are the leaders of their governments.

4. England has a red, white, and blue _____. It flies on top of the palace.

5. The queen lives on the second level of the palace. She lives on the second

   _____.

6. The queen sometimes gets a very important telephone call. Sometimes the call is an _____.

7. The queen puts the dogs' food in round dishes. She puts it in

   _____.

WORDS THAT GO TOGETHER

Write the correct words in the blanks.

follow rules	the rest of	a lot of	on top of

1. The queen works in her office for one part of the day. Then she goes to other places for _____ the day.

2. Many people meet the queen. _____ people go to her garden parties.

3. There is a flag _____ Buckingham Palace. It is the highest part of the palace.

4. At dinner with the queen, you must _____. There are some things you are allowed to do and other things you are not allowed to do.

USE

Work with a partner to answer the questions. Use complete sentences.

1. What do you put in *bowls*?
2. What do you see *a lot of* on the street?
3. What are the colors of your country's *flag*?
4. What *floor* is your classroom on?
5. Who *prepares* your dinner?
6. Who is a famous *politician*?
7. When there is an *emergency*, like a fire, what do you do?

COMPREHENSION

UNDERSTANDING THE READING

Circle the letter of the correct answer.

1. Buckingham Palace is _____.
   a. near a small town   b. a new building   c. the home of the queen

2. Buckingham Palace is _____.
   a. like a town   b. famous for its flag   c. a small palace

3. You can visit Buckingham Palace _____.
   a. all year   b. in August and September   c. when the queen is there

REMEMBERING DETAILS

Reread the passage and answer the questions.

1. Where is Buckingham Palace?
2. What floor does the queen live on?
3. When does the queen have garden parties?
4. How many people does she invite?
5. How many rooms does the palace have?
6. When does the queen start her day?
7. What does the queen do after lunch?

SENTENCE COMPLETION

Match the words in Column A and Column B to make sentences.

A

____ 1. The queen visits

____ 2. The queen has breakfast

____ 3. The queen never answers

____ 4. The queen works

____ 5. Visitors can go

____ 6. The queen meets

B

a. the telephone during dinner.

b. hospitals, schools, or new buildings.

c. in her office in the morning.

d. at 8:30 in the morning.

e. a lot of people.

f. to the palace in August and September.

DICTATION

Work with a partner. Read three sentences from the exercise above. Your partner listens and writes the sentences. Then your partner reads three sentences and you write them.

DISCUSSION

Discuss the answers to these questions with your classmates.

1. Do you think the queen has a wonderful life? Give reasons.
2. Do countries need kings and queens?
3. What other countries have kings or queens? What are they like? What do they do?

WRITING

Complete the sentences about Buckingham Palace and the queen.

Example: The queen lives in Buckingham Palace. _____

1. Buckingham Palace was built _____
2. Buckingham Palace is _____
3. Buckingham Palace has _____
4. The queen has breakfast _____
5. After lunch, the queen visits _____

Spelling and Punctuation

WORDS WITH *QU*

> We spell the /kw/ sound *qu* in most English words. Never use *q* alone.
> Always use *qu*. A vowel (*a, e, i, o,* or *u*) always follows *qu*.
>
> | | | | |
> |---|---|---|---|
> | **qu**een | **qu**iet | s**qu**eeze | e**qu**al |
> | **qu**ality | ban**qu**et | **qu**estion | **qu**ick |

A. Circle the correctly spelled word in each group. You may use a dictionary.

1. quiz   quuiz   qwiz
2. earthkwake   earthkuake   earthquake

3. skuare   square   scquare
4. qwote   quote   qote

B. Underline the misspelled words. Write the correct words on the lines.

1. The qween lives in the palace.   _____

2. It is qiet in the palace.   _____

3. She gives many banqwets.   _____

4. You must never skeeze her hand.   _____

5. Guests eat kwality food.   _____

6. She doesn't eat qwuickly.   _____

7. A guest never asks her a qwestion.   _____

8. She acwuaints herself with her guests.   _____

9. There are skwuirrels in the palace garden.   _____

10. There are also ducks. They qwack.   _____

UNIT 4

Why Are Cows Special in India?

BEFORE YOU READ

Answer these questions.

1. What do you know about cows?
2. Why are the cows in the street?
3. Where do you see cows in your country?

Why Are Cows Special in India?

1 About one billion people live in India. Many people live on small **farms**. They live a quiet and **simple** life. The family takes care of the farm and the animals. The most important animal on the farm is the cow. The cow helps on the farm in two ways. It gives milk to the family, and it works on the farm.

2 The farmers do not make a lot of money. They can't buy machines to help them do their work. Also, the weather is a **problem** in India. In June, July, August, and September, there's a lot of rain. The **ground** gets very wet. Then the ground gets **soft**. A machine cannot work on soft ground, but a cow can work. Cows also do not **cost** a lot of money. They don't need gasoline or **repairs** like machines.

3 Farmers care about their cows very much. They want their cows to be happy. The farms aren't busy at certain times of the year. At these times, people wash and **decorate** their cows. Americans like to wash their cars, and Indians like to wash their cows! Two times a year, there are special celebrations for the cows. These celebrations are like Thanksgiving in the United States.

4 Old cows cannot work on farms. In India, it is **against the law** to kill a cow. So farmers send their old cows away from the farm. The cows walk around free in the streets. Sometimes men sell grass in the street. People buy the grass and give it to the cows. People also give their own food to the cows, and cars are careful not to **hit** the cows. There are special animal hospitals for old or sick cows. The government and some rich people pay for these hospitals.

5 People in other countries do not understand why the Indian government **spends money on** cows. There are many poor people in India who need money. Indians say that Americans spend more money on cats and dogs. People in India care for over 200 million cows every year. They have cared for cows **for a long time**. It is a tradition that is thousands of years old.

VOCABULARY

MEANING

Write the correct words in the blanks.

farms	cost	problem	decorate	soft
repairs	ground	simple	hit	

1. The farmers do not do special things. They have a _____ life.
2. Cows live on land where people grow food and keep animals. They live on _____.
3. The land we walk on is called the _____.
4. The ground is _____. It is not hard.
5. Cows do not _____ a lot of money. They have a low price.
6. The car doesn't work. It needs _____.
7. In July, it rains a lot. It is bad for the land. The rain is a _____.
8. Drivers do not want to _____ cows. They do not want to hurt the cows.
9. People put things on their cows. They want the cows to look nice. They _____ the cows.

WORDS THAT GO TOGETHER

Write the correct words in the blanks.

for a long time	spends money on	against the law

1. People are not allowed to kill cows in India. It is _____.
2. In India, the government _____ its cows. The government pays for many things for the cows.
3. Indians have loved cows for many years. They have cared about them _____.

USE

Work with a partner to answer the questions. Use complete sentences.

1. What do you *spend* a lot of *money on*?
2. What is *against the law* in your country?
3. What is something that is *soft*?
4. What animals do you see on *farms*?
5. What *repairs* do you do in your home?
6. What is a *problem* you have in English?

COMPREHENSION

UNDERSTANDING THE READING

Circle the letter of the correct answer.

1. Cows help farmers because cows _____.
   a. work on farms   b. walk around the streets   c. eat grass

2. In India, people do not _____.
   a. kill cows   b. take care of cows   c. have hospitals for cows

3. In India, the government spends money on _____.
   a. poor people   b. farms   c. cows

REMEMBERING DETAILS

Circle *T* if the sentence is true. Circle *F* if the sentence is false.

1.	In India, there is one celebration for the cows every year.	T	F
2.	Indians take care of 20 million cows every year.	T	F
3.	People buy grass and give it to the cows.	T	F
4.	Indians wash and decorate their cows every day.	T	F
5.	Indians spend money on cats and dogs.	T	F
6.	Farmers want their cows to be happy.	T	F

SENTENCE COMPLETION

Match the words in Column A and Column B to make sentences.

	A	**B**
____ 1.	Indians want	a. free in the streets.
____ 2.	The government pays for	b. their cows to be happy.
____ 3.	An old cow walks	c. special animal hospitals.
____ 4.	Cows give milk and	d. after it rains.
____ 5.	Farmers don't have	e. work on small farms.
____ 6.	Machines cannot work	f. money to buy machines.

DICTATION

Work with a partner. Read three sentences from the exercise above. Your partner listens and writes the sentences. Then your partner reads three sentences and you write them.

DISCUSSION

Discuss the answers to these questions with your classmates.

1. The Indian government spends a lot of money on cows. Is this a good idea? Explain.
2. What animal has a special meaning in your country?
3. The cow celebration is special in India. What is a special celebration in your country?

WRITING

Complete the sentences about cows.

Example: Cows work on farms. _____

1. Cows give _____
2. Farmers use cows _____
3. In India, an old cow cannot _____
4. People in other countries do not understand _____
5. People in India care for _____

SPELLING AND PUNCTUATION

APOSTROPHES: CONTRACTIONS

> We use an apostrophe (') in a contraction. *Contractions* are words with missing letters. We use the apostrophe in place of the missing letters.
>
> *The farms **are not** busy at certain times of the year.*
> *= The farms **aren't** busy at certain times of the year.*
>
> ***There is** a lot of rain.*
> *= **There's** a lot of rain.*

Underline the words that need apostrophes for contractions. Write the correct contractions on the lines. One sentence has two contractions. The first one is done for you.

1. Farmers <u>do not</u> make a lot of money.   *don't*

2. They cannot buy machines.   _____

3. Cows do not need repairs.   _____

4. In India, it is important to care for cows.   _____

5. The ground is not hard.   _____

6. Old cows cannot work on farms.   _____

7. In India, they are careful not to hit cows.   _____

8. There is a cow hospital in the town.   _____

9. People do not understand why Indians spend money on cows.   _____

10. It is a tradition that is thousands of years old.   _____

UNIT 5

How Do Mexicans Celebrate the Day of the Dead?

BEFORE YOU READ

Answer these questions.

1. What are the people doing?
2. What are they wearing?
3. Are the people happy?

How Do Mexicans Celebrate the Day of the Dead?

1 At the end of October, Mexicans prepare to celebrate the Day of the Dead. The Day of the Dead celebration is two days: November 1 and November 2. On these days, Mexicans **remember** their dead friends and relatives. Relatives are people in your family.

2 People are not sad on the Day of the Dead. They are happy. Markets and shops sell special things before the Day of the Dead. They sell **candles**, flowers, candies, and chocolates that look like skulls or **bones**. They also sell bread called Bread of the Dead. The bread looks like skulls or bones, too!

3 Families believe that their dead relatives and friends are going to visit them. They make an altar in their home for their dead visitors. An altar is a special table with pictures of the dead person. People put flowers, candles, and some of the dead person's **favorite** things on the altar. The family also puts the dead person's favorite food and drinks there. People leave many different kinds of food and drinks: coffee, water, rice and beans, chicken, fruit, and the special bread and candies for the Day of the Dead. The family also leaves a bowl with water and a clean **towel**. This is for the dead visitors to wash their hands before the **meal**. Then the family lights the candles and waits for the dead person to visit them.

4 At **midnight**, the family leaves the house. They go to the graves of their relatives. A grave is the place in the ground where people put a dead body. The family cleans the grave. They also decorate it with flowers and candles. Then they **have a picnic** on the grave with special food and drinks. They **tell stories** about the dead person and talk to the dead person. They eat, drink, play music, and sing.

5 Different parts of Mexico have different Day of the Dead traditions. Today, in many big towns, Mexican families **get together** to have a special dinner at home. They eat the Bread of the Dead at this meal. The Bread of the Dead has a toy **skeleton** in it. The Mexicans believe that the person who gets the toy skeleton will have good luck.

VOCABULARY

MEANING

Write the correct words in the blanks.

| candles | meal | midnight | favorite |
| remember | bones | skeleton | towel |

1. Mexicans think about people from the past on the Day of the Dead. They _____ them.
2. Mexicans put _____ at the grave. They want light at the grave.
3. The family eats a special _____. They sit together at the table and eat and drink.
4. The visitors wash their hands with water. Then they dry them with a _____.
5. His _____ food is chicken. He likes it more than all other food.
6. My mother fell. She broke two _____ in her arm.
7. They went to the cemetery at 12 o'clock at night. It was _____.
8. All the bones of a person are called a _____.

WORDS THAT GO TOGETHER

Write the correct words in the blanks.

| get together | have a picnic | tell stories |

1. At the cemetery, they eat food and have drinks. They _____.
2. They remember the dead person and _____ about the person.
3. His family likes to _____ on the Day of the Dead. They meet and do something special.

How Do Mexicans Celebrate the Day of the Dead?   27

USE

Work with a partner to answer the questions. Use complete sentences.

1. Where do you *have a picnic*?
2. When do you burn *candles*?
3. Who is your *favorite* relative?
4. When do eat your big *meal*?
5. Where do you usually *get together* with friends?
6. Where do you put *towels*?

COMPREHENSION

UNDERSTANDING THE READING

Circle the letter of the correct answer.

1. The Day of the Dead is _____.
   a. a time to be sad   b. a time to remember   c. at the end of
                                dead friends and relatives   October

2. At home, the family puts things on a special _____ for the dead
   person.
   a. table   b. candle   c. grave

3. At midnight, the family goes to _____.
   a. the market   b. the dead person's home   c. the cemetery

REMEMBERING DETAILS

Circle *T* if the sentence is true. Circle *F* if the sentence is false.

1. The Day of the Dead celebration is for one day.   T   F

2. They sell bread called Food of the Dead.   T   F

3. People put food and drinks on the altar.   T   F

4. At midnight, the family goes to their house.   T   F

5. The family decorates the grave with flowers   T   F
   and candles.

6. The person with the toy skeleton will have good luck.   T   F

UNDERSTANDING THE SEQUENCE

Which happened first? Write *1* on the line. Which happened second? Write *2* on the line.

1. _____ The markets sell flowers, candles, and special candy.

   _____ Mexicans celebrate the Day of the Dead on November 1 and November 2.

2. _____ The family waits for the dead person to visit them.

   _____ The family makes an altar for the dead visitors.

3. _____ The family cleans and decorates the grave.

   _____ At midnight, the family leaves the house.

4. _____ The family eats, drinks, plays music, and sings.

   _____ The family has a picnic.

TELL THE STORY

Work with a partner. Tell the story of the Day of the Dead to your partner. Use your own words. Your partner asks you questions about the story. Then your partner tells you the story and you ask questions.

DISCUSSION

Discuss the answers to these questions with your classmates.

1. Why are people happy on the Day of the Dead?
2. How do people remember the dead in your country?
3. Do you believe dead people come back and visit? Why or why not?

WRITING

Complete the sentences about the Day of the Dead.

Example: Mexicans celebrate _the Day of the Dead._ _____

1. The Day of the Dead is _____
2. The markets and shops sell _____
3. Families believe _____
4. At midnight, _____
5. In big towns, Mexican families _____

SPELLING AND PUNCTUATION

 COMMAS: ITEMS IN A SERIES

> **We use a comma between words or phrases in a series of three or more.**
>
> *The shops sell **candles, flowers, candies,** and **chocolates.***
>
> **We do <u>not</u> use a comma between two words or phrases in a series.**
>
> *Mexicans remember their dead **relatives** and **friends.***

Put commas in the correct places. Three sentences do not need commas.

1. The markets and shops sell candies.
2. People dress up as ghosts mummies and skeletons.
3. They decorate homes and parks for the holiday.
4. On the table, there are flowers candles fruits and photos.
5. A favorite thing is a book letter ring or watch.
6. There is a bowl soap and towel for the dead visitor.
7. They go to the cemetery with flowers candles and blankets.
8. People clean wash and decorate the grave.
9. Some bring guitars and radios.
10. They eat drink and sing.

UNIT 6

Who Are the Inuit?

BEFORE YOU READ

Answer these questions.

1. What is the man doing?
2. What do you think he eats?
3. Does he like where he lives?

Who Are the Inuit?

1 The Inuit are special people. The old name for Inuit was "Eskimo." *Eskimo* means "eater of meat." In 1977, the Eskimos changed their name to "Inuit." *Inuit* means "the people" in their language. They live in very cold places: Siberia, Alaska, Canada, and Greenland. These are the coldest parts of the world.

2 There are about 120,000 Inuit in the world today. Canada has 20,000 Inuit. Some live very close to the North Pole. The Inuit were the first people of Canada.

3 In the past, the Inuit hunted for all their food. The men traveled in the snow on sleds. About ten dogs **pulled** a sled. The men killed fish and other animals. Then they went home and **shared** their food with other families. The Inuit used every part of the animal for food and clothes. They usually ate the fish **raw**. The women made clothes from animal **skins**. They made shoes from the skins, too. The Inuit had an old **custom**. The women **chewed** their husbands' shoes at night. Then the shoes were soft in the morning.

4 The Inuit's life was **hard**. They lived in houses made of snow. They moved **from time to time** to hunt animals. Sometimes, the Inuit needed money. Other Canadians needed animal skins. The Inuit sold animal skins to these Canadians. The Inuit and the Canadians helped **each other**.

5 Today in Canada, the Inuit's lives are very different. Most Inuit live in villages. The villages have from 300 to 1,500 people. The houses are made of **wood**. The Inuit don't travel in sleds. They ride snowmobiles. They buy food and clothes from stores.

6 The Inuit **keep in touch with** the rest of the world. They use the telephone, television, and the Internet. They go on airplanes to cities in the south of Canada. Inuit boys and girls go to school and have Inuit teachers. They learn about the world. **At the same time**, the Inuit want to remember their language and traditions. They want to teach their language and traditions to their children.

7 In the 1970s, the Inuit in Canada wanted to **control** their land. In 1999, the Canadian government agreed. The government gave the Inuit a piece of land in the north of Canada. The name of the Inuit's new land is *Nunavut*. It means "our land" in their language.

VOCABULARY

MEANING

Write the correct words in the blanks.

shared	control	chewed	raw	wood
pulled	custom	hard	skins	

1. One Inuit family did not eat all the food. They _____ the food with other families.
2. The men tied a rope from the dogs to the sled. Then the dogs _____ the sled in the snow.
3. The women put the animal skin in their mouth. Then they moved their teeth up and down. They _____ the skin.
4. They did not cook the fish. They ate it _____.
5. Some things are difficult for the Inuit. Their lives are _____.
6. The women used the outside part of the dead animal. They made clothes from the _____.
7. The Inuit wanted to _____ their land. They did not want the Canadians to tell them what to do.
8. All Inuit women have a special way to fix the shoes. It is a _____.
9. The Inuit men cut trees. They used the _____ to make houses.

WORDS THAT GO TOGETHER

Write the correct words in the blanks.

at the same time	each other
keep in touch with	from time to time

1. The Inuit helped the Canadians, and the Canadians helped the Inuit. They helped _____.
2. Sometimes the Inuit went to a new place. They went _____.
3. The teacher taught two things together. She taught different things _____.
4. The Inuit want to _____ other people. They send e-mails and make telephone calls.

USE

Work with a partner to answer the questions. Use complete sentences.

1. What kind of food do you eat *raw*?
2. What is something you *chew* for a long time?
3. What is something people *share*?
4. What is an interesting *custom* from your country?
5. How do you *keep in touch with* your friends?
6. What two things do you do *at the same time*?

COMPREHENSION

UNDERSTANDING THE READING

Circle the letter of the correct answer.

1. The Inuit _____.
   a. live all over the world   b. live in cold places   c. don't eat meat

2. In the past, the Inuit _____.
   a. hunted animals   b. lived in wood houses   c. bought clothes
      for food   in stores

3. Today the Inuit _____.
   a. travel in sleds   b. make shoes from skins   c. learn all about the world

REMEMBERING DETAILS

Reread the passage and answer the questions.

1. Where do the Inuit live?
2. How many Inuit are there today?
3. What does the word *Eskimo* mean?
4. How did the men travel in the past?
5. Where do the Inuit get food today?
6. What is the name of the new land for the Canadian Inuit?

SENTENCE COMPLETION

Match the words in Column A and Column B to make sentences.

A	B
____ 1. The Inuit hunted	a. clothes from animal skins.
____ 2. In the past, the Inuit moved	b. in villages.
____ 3. The women made	c. food and clothes from stores.
____ 4. Today the Inuit live	d. from time to time to hunt.
____ 5. The Canadian government gave	e. fish and animals for food.
____ 6. Today the Inuit buy	f. the Inuit a piece of land.

DICTATION

Work with a partner. Read three sentences from the exercise above. Your partner listens and writes the sentences. Then your partner reads three sentences and you write them.

DISCUSSION

Discuss the answers to these questions with your classmates.

1. Life today is easy for many people, but it is expensive. In the past, people did not spend a lot of money to buy things. Which is better: life today or life in the past? Explain.
2. Would you like to live in a very cold place or a very hot place? Why?
3. In the past, the Inuit wore animal skins. Today some people do not wear animal skins. What do you think about wearing animal skins?

WRITING

Complete the sentences about the Inuit.

Example: The Inuit live _in Siberia, Alaska, Canada, and Greenland._

1. In 1977, the Eskimos _____
2. In the past, the Inuit _____
3. The Inuit men _____
4. The Inuit women _____
5. Today the Inuit _____

SPELLING AND PUNCTUATION

PLURALS: NOUNS ENDING IN -Y

Some singular nouns end in –y. Look at the letter before the –y.

If the letter is a vowel, add –s.

boy—boys   day—days

If the letter is a consonant, change the –y to –i, and add –es.

family—families   city—cities

A. Circle the correctly spelled word in each group. You may use a dictionary.

1. holidays   holidaies   holidayes
2. ladyies   ladies   ladys

3. highwaies   highways   highwayes
4. flyies   flys   flies

B. Underline the misspelled words. Write the correct words on the lines.

1. The Inuit like to tell storys.   _____

2. Inuit babyes like the snow.   _____

3. The snow houses did not have keies.   _____

4. They hunted animals for food for their
   familyes.   _____

5. The boyies learn to hunt from their fathers.   _____

6. Three new companyies opened in the Inuit
   village.   _____

7. There are librarys in many Inuit towns.   _____

8. Inuit children have fun on their birthdaies.   _____

9. They have partys like other children.   _____

10. In the past, they made toyies from fish bones. _____

UNIT 7

What Is Beatlemania?

BEFORE YOU READ

Answer these questions.

1. What are the Beatles' names?
2. When did the Beatles start?
3. What Beatles songs do you know?

What Is Beatlemania?

1 Beatlemania is a very strong feeling for the **group**, the Beatles. The Beatles were four young musicians from Liverpool, England. Their names were John Lennon, Paul McCartney, George Harrison, and Ringo Starr. These four men never took music lessons. They **taught themselves** to play music.

2 In 1957, John started a group called the Quarrymen. He was sixteen years old. Then he met Paul. They began to write songs and sing **together**. Soon, George **joined** them. The group started to play in England and make money. They went to Germany and played **concerts** there, too. The group had different names. They also had some different musicians. In 1962, Ringo joined them. Then John, Paul, George, and Ringo were the Beatles.

3 The Beatles made their first **hit** song in 1962. The song was "Love Me Do." In 1963, their song "Please Please Me" was a bigger hit. **In all**, they had twenty-nine hit songs. By 1963, the Beatles were very popular in England, and Beatlemania started. They had many **fans**. Their fans **screamed** and cried. At concerts, their fans screamed very, very loudly. The Beatles could not hear themselves sing!

4 The next year, the Beatles went to the United States. The Americans loved them, and Beatlemania started in America, too. People everywhere **copied** their clothes and their hair. The Beatles were the most popular rock-and-roll group **in the world**.

5 The Beatles **broke up** in 1970. They wanted to play new music. All of the Beatles did interesting, new things. John wrote music with his wife, Yoko Ono. Paul started a new group called Wings with his wife, Linda. George and Ringo made their own records and gave concerts. Sadly, John was shot dead in New York in 1980. He was forty years old. George became sick and died in 2001.

6 We still hear Beatles songs on the radio today. Their music and songs will never die.

VOCABULARY

MEANING

Write the correct words in the blanks.

group	hit	fans	screamed
concerts	copied	together	joined

1. John and Paul wrote songs with each other. They wrote songs

   _____.

2. People wanted to look like the Beatles. They _____ their clothes and hair.

3. The song "Love Me Do" was very popular. It was a _____ song.

4. The Beatles went to different places and played music for a lot of people. They gave _____.

5. Many people loved the Beatles and their music. These people were

   _____.

6. At Beatles concerts, people made a lot of noise. They _____.

7. The Beatles were a famous singing _____. The four Beatles sang together.

8. Ringo wanted to be part of the Beatles. He _____ the Beatles.

WORDS THAT GO TOGETHER

Write the correct words in the blanks.

broke up	in all	in the world	taught themselves

1. People everywhere loved the Beatles. They were the most popular group

   _____.

2. Nobody helped the Beatles learn music. They _____ to play music.

3. In 1970, the Beatles _____. They stopped playing music together.

4. The total number of Beatles songs was twenty-nine. They had twenty-nine hit songs _____.

USE

Work with a partner to answer the questions. Use complete sentences.

1. What is the name of a famous singing *group*?
2. What is the name of a *hit* song?
3. Who is the most popular singer or group *in the world* now?
4. How many students are in your class *in all*?
5. Which singer or group are you a *fan* of?
6. What does your class do *together*?

COMPREHENSION

UNDERSTANDING THE READING

Circle the letter of the correct answer.

1. The Beatles made their first hit song _____.
   a. in England b. in Germany c. in the United States

2. John started the Quarrymen. Then he met _____.
   a. George b. Paul c. Ringo

3. In 1970, the Beatles _____.
   a. went to the United States b. broke up c. gave concerts

REMEMBERING DETAILS

Reread the passage and answer the questions.

1. How many Beatles were there?
2. Where were the Beatles from?
3. How many hit songs did the Beatles have?
4. Where did Beatlemania start?
5. What did people copy from the Beatles?
6. Why did the Beatles break up?
7. When did John Lennon die?

UNDERSTANDING THE SEQUENCE

Which happened first? Write *1* on the line. Which happened second? Write *2* on the line.

1. _____ Ringo joined the group.

   _____ The group became the Beatles.

2. _____ The song "Love Me Do" was a hit.

   _____ The song "Please Please Me" was a hit.

3. _____ Beatlemania started in England.

   _____ The Beatles went to America.

4. _____ Paul McCartney started a new group.

   _____ The Beatles broke up.

TELL THE STORY

Work with a partner. Tell the story of the Beatles to your partner. Use your own words. Your partner asks you questions about the story. Then your partner tells you the story and you ask questions.

DISCUSSION

Discuss the answers to these questions with your classmates.

1. What kind of music is popular in your country now?
2. Who is your favorite singer or musical group?
3. The Beatles' music is over forty years old. What are some other popular old songs?

WRITING

Complete the sentences about the Beatles.

Example: The Beatles were <u>from England.</u> _____

1. The Beatles were _____
2. The Beatles made _____
3. By 1963, the Beatles had _____
4. In 1964, the Beatles went _____
5. The Beatles broke up because _____

SPELLING AND PUNCTUATION

VERBS WITH –ED OR –ING

Many verbs end in –e. We usually drop the –e before we add –ed or –ing.

love + ed = loved   *Everybody **lov**ed the Beatles.*
write + ing = writing   *John and Paul were **writ**ing many songs.*

A. Circle the correctly spelled word for each sentence. You may use a dictionary.

1. The 1960s was an (exciting/exciteing) time for music.
2. John and Paul were (composeing/composing) many of the songs.
3. The Beatles were (invited/inviteed) to meet the queen.
4. At one time, the Beatles (moved/movied) to Germany.
5. The Beatles (lived/liveed) in Liverpool when they were young.
6. They were (hoping/hopeing) to be popular in America.
7. Their fans were (comeing/coming) from all over the country to see them.
8. The Beatles (continueed/continued) to be popular for years.
9. Their songs were (translated/translateed) to other languages.
10. The music of the Beatles has (surviveed/survived) for more than 40 years.

B. Write three new verbs that end in –e. Then add –ed and –ing to them. You may use a dictionary.

Verb	–ed	–ing
1. _____	_____	_____
2. _____	_____	_____
3. _____	_____	_____

UNIT 8

Where Is the Great Wall?

BEFORE YOU READ

Answer these questions.

1. What do you know about the Great Wall?
2. How big is it?
3. Why is it called "Great"?

Where Is the Great Wall?

1 The Great Wall is in China. The Chinese built the Great Wall thousands of years ago. They wanted to **protect** their country from unfriendly people. First, they built small walls around their towns. Then the emperor, Shi Huangdi, joined the walls and built new parts. He wanted to make one long wall—the Great Wall.

2 Shi Huangdi was the first Qin emperor. The name *Qin* sounds like *Chin*. The word *China* **comes from** the name *Qin*. Shi Huangdi made many changes in China. He wanted China to be strong and **modern**. But many Chinese did not like Shi Huangdi. He didn't **care about** the people. Many people died because of his changes. Thousands of men worked on the Great Wall. It was very hard work. Many men got sick and died. Over one million people died to make the wall. Their bodies are **buried** in the wall. Some people say the Great Wall is "the Wall of Death."

3 Other Chinese emperors **added** to the wall and made it better. The Ming emperors added thousands of tall, strong buildings in the years 1368–1644. Men stayed in the buildings to protect and repair the wall. They were called guards. Sometimes more than a million guards worked on the wall. They were born on the wall and **grew up** there. They married there and died there. Many guards lived on the Great Wall all their lives. Sometimes unfriendly men came to the wall to start problems. The guards made a fire to show they needed help. Guards from other parts of the wall ran **along** the top of the wall to help them.

4 We don't know **exactly** how long the Great Wall is. There are many different parts of the wall, and some parts **fell down**. The wall is about 4,000 miles (6,400 kilometers) long and about 25 feet (7.6 meters) high. It is about 15 feet (4.6 meters) wide at the top. Buses and cars can drive along it. Today, the Great Wall is the largest **structure** in the world. Some people say you can see the Great Wall from **space**. But in 1969, an astronaut who traveled in space said he did not see any buildings—not even the Great Wall.

Vocabulary

MEANING

Write the correct words in the blanks.

added	protect	buried	space
exactly	modern	structure	along

1. The Chinese did not want unfriendly people in their country. They wanted to _____ their country.

2. How long is the Great Wall? We don't know the complete answer. We don't know _____ how long it is.

3. Other emperors put new parts onto the Great Wall. They _____ to it.

4. The emperor wanted China to be _____. He wanted China to have new things and new ideas.

5. An astronaut in _____ did not see the Great Wall. He was very far up in the sky away from the Earth.

6. The Chinese built something very big. They built a big _____.

7. You can drive a car or bus from one end of the wall to the other. You can drive _____ the top of the wall.

8. The stones and rocks in the wall covered some men's bodies. The bodies were _____.

WORDS THAT GO TOGETHER

Write the correct words in the blanks.

care about	comes from	fell down	grew up

1. Some parts of the wall _____. The parts dropped to the ground.

2. Some words are developed from other words. The word *China* _____ the name *Qin*.

3. Many guards lived on the wall as children. They stayed there and became adults. They _____ on the wall.

4. The emperor was not interested in his people. He did not _____ them.

USE

Work with a partner to answer the questions. Use complete sentences.

1. What is a big *structure* in your country?
2. Where did you *grow up*?
3. What *protects* you from the rain?
4. What can you see in *space*?
5. Who do you *care about* very much?
6. When *exactly* did you move to your home?

COMPREHENSION

UNDERSTANDING THE READING

Circle the letter of the correct answer.

1. China's first Qin emperor _____.
   a. joined the small walls
   b. put a million guards at the wall
   c. made the first small wall

2. Guards protected the wall from _____.
   a. unfriendly men
   b. the emperor
   c. other guards

3. An astronaut in space _____.
   a. saw part of the wall
   b. saw the whole wall
   c. did not see the wall

REMEMBERING DETAILS

Circle *T* if the sentence is true. Circle *F* if the sentence is false.

1. The Ming emperors made the first wall.   T   F
2. The word *China* comes from the name of the first Qin emperor.   T   F
3. Over a million people died to make the wall.   T   F
4. Guards protected and repaired the wall.   T   F
5. A bus can drive along the top of the wall.   T   F
6. The wall is about 400 miles long.   T   F

SENTENCE COMPLETION

Match the words in Column A and Column B to make sentences.

A	B
____ 1. The Great Wall is	a. many changes in China.
____ 2. Many guards lived	b. the largest structure in the world
____ 3. The first emperor made	c. on the wall all their lives.
____ 4. The Chinese wanted	d. thousands of tall, strong buildings.
____ 5. Sometimes unfriendly men came	e. to protect their country.
____ 6. The Ming emperors added	f. to the wall to start problems.

DICTATION

Work with a partner. Read three sentences from the exercise above. Your partner listens and writes the sentences. Then your partner reads three sentences and you write them.

DISCUSSION

Discuss the answers to these questions with your classmates.

1. What is the biggest structure or building in your country?
2. Many important buildings are big. Some important buildings are small. What is a small, important building?
3. Do you like new buildings or old buildings? Why?

WRITING

Complete the sentences about the Great Wall.

Example: The Great Wall is _in China._ _____

1. The Chinese built _____
2. Shi Huangdi _____
3. Emperors added _____
4. Many guards _____
5. Today the Great Wall is _____

SPELLING AND PUNCTUATION

 ## CAPITAL LETTERS: IMPORTANT STRUCTURES AND MONUMENTS

We use a capital letter for the main words in the name of an important structure or monument. We do <u>not</u> use a capital letter for the words *the* or *of* in the name.

*Some people say the **G**reat **W**all is the **W**all of **D**eath.*

Underline the words that need capital letters. Remember the capital letter rules from other units.

1. In beijing, china, the temple of heaven is one of the most beautiful sights.
2. The largest palace in china is called the forbidden city.
3. The tallest buildings in the world are the petronas towers in kuala lumpur, malaysia.
4. The largest castle in the world is prague castle in the czech republic.
5. The largest and oldest castle which people use is windsor castle near london in england.
6. At one time, the eiffel tower in paris, france, was the tallest structure in the world.
7. Later, the empire state building in new york became the tallest structure.
8. In 1976, the CN tower in toronto, canada, became the tallest tower in the world.
9. The gateway arch in saint louis, missouri, is the highest monument in the world.
10. The tallest statue in the world is amida buddha in ushiku city, japan.

UNIT 9

Why Do People Give Gifts for Weddings?

BEFORE YOU READ

Answer these questions.

1. What kinds of gifts do people give at weddings in your country?
2. What do the parents of the woman give?
3. What do the parents of the man give?

Why Do People Give Gifts for Weddings?

1   People give gifts for weddings for different **reasons**. Usually, people want to help the **bride** and **groom**. Many countries have their own customs. In the United States, both families give gifts to the **couple**. In other places, the customs are very different.

2   In India, the groom's family **asks for** a large payment from the bride's family. The payment is called a *dowry*. Sometimes the payment is a special gift with a **brand name**. For example, some families ask for a Singer sewing machine or a Sony television set. Sometimes the payment is money. The money may be equal to the family's **salary** for two or three years. Both families **agree** about the money. They agree on how much money the bride's family can **afford** to pay. Some Indian families do not like to have many daughters. It is too expensive! Today in India, a woman with a large salary is **the same as** a woman with a large dowry.

3   In the Middle East, the bride's family asks for a large amount of money from the groom. The gift is called a *mahr*. The *mahr* is money and sometimes land or a home. In Saudi Arabia, the groom gives a lot of money. He buys clothes for the bride for one year and buys furniture for their new home. Rich couples get **expensive** gifts from both parents. The parents often give nice furniture or a new car.

4   At one time in Saudi Arabia, the *mahr* for a bride was very, very high. Men could not afford to marry Saudi Arabian women. They married women from Lebanon and Egypt. This was bad for Saudi women. Soon, many Saudi women did not have husbands. The government made new rules. They made it hard to marry a **foreigner**. Another Middle Eastern country, Oman, had problems, too. Soldiers in the army could not afford to get married. The sultan of Oman made a law against large *mahr* payments. This helped couples in Oman to get married.

5   A wedding is a very special and important time. People give gifts for different reasons, but one thing is the same. Everybody wants to help the bride and groom start a happy life together.

VOCABULARY

MEANING

Write the correct words in the blanks.

bride	groom	foreigner	agree	afford
couple	expensive	reasons	salary	

1. A man and a woman who are getting married are the _____.
2. The woman who is getting married is the _____.
3. The man who is getting married is the _____.
4. Some families give all the money they get from their jobs to the groom's family. They give their _____.
5. The man did not marry a woman from his country. He married a

    _____.
6. Why did the sultan make a new law? What were the _____ why he made the law?
7. The wedding gift was _____. It cost a lot of money.
8. The two families have the same ideas about the wedding gift. They _____ about the wedding gift.
9. The family had enough money to buy the gift. They could _____ the gift.

WORDS THAT GO TOGETHER

Write the correct words in the blanks.

brand name	the same as	asks for

1. The groom's family wants special things. The family _____ the things they want.
2. A large salary for a woman is _____ a large dowry. They are like each other in many ways.
3. People give gifts from famous companies. The gifts have a

    _____.

USE

Work with a partner to answer the questions. Use complete sentences.

1. What is a *brand name* of clothes you like?
2. What color dress does a *bride* wear in your country?
3. What does a *groom* wear in your country?
4. What does the *couple* do after the wedding ceremony?
5. When can you *afford* to go on a trip?
6. What are some *reasons* to get married?
7. What problems does a *foreigner* have in a new country?

COMPREHENSION

UNDERSTANDING THE READING

Circle the letter of the correct answer.

1. Wedding gift customs are _____.
   a. the same all over the world   b. the same in India and the Middle East   c. different in most countries

2. In India, the groom's family _____.
   a. gives payment   b. asks for payment   c. asks for furniture

3. In Saudi Arabia, the groom _____.
   a. gives payment   b. wants a foreign bride   c. asks for payment

REMEMBERING DETAILS

Circle *T* if the sentence is true. Circle *F* if the sentence is false.

1. In the United States, the parents of the bride and groom give gifts.	T	F
2. Indian families like to have many daughters.	T	F
3. In the Middle East, the gift for a bride is a *mahr*.	T	F
4. At one time, many Saudi women did not have husbands.	T	F
5. The men from Saudi Arabia married women from Oman.	T	F
6. In Oman, the sultan could not afford to get married.	T	F

SENTENCE COMPLETION

Match the words in Column A and Column B to make sentences.

A	**B**
_____ 1. Many countries have	a. the couple start a happy life.
_____ 2. Gifts help	b. their own customs.
_____ 3. In the Middle East, the groom	c. very high at one time.
_____ 4. The *mahr* was	d. gives money and land or a home.
_____ 5. In India, the bride's family	e. the same as a woman with a large salary.
_____ 6. A large dowry is	f. sometimes gives gifts with brand names.

DICTATION

Work with a partner. Read three sentences from the exercise above. Your partner listens and writes the sentences. Then your partner reads three sentences and you write them.

DISCUSSION

Discuss the answers to these questions with your classmates.

1. Who pays for weddings in your country?
2. Do you think the custom of giving wedding gifts in your country is good? Why or why not?
3. Some countries have arranged marriages. Do you think this is a good idea?

WRITING

Complete the sentences about wedding gifts.

Example: Each country has its own customs. _____

1. In the United States, _____
2. In India, _____
3. In Saudi Arabia, _____
4. In Oman, _____
5. People give gifts _____

SPELLING AND PUNCTUATION

 CAPITAL LETTERS: BRAND NAMES

We use a capital letter for the brand name of a product.

*They like **S**inger sewing machines.*

We do **not** use a capital letter for a product with no special name.

They use sewing machines to make clothes.

A. Circle the correctly spelled words for each sentence.

1. The girl's parents are going to buy her a (Dior suit/dior suit).
2. The bride will have a special (wedding dress/Wedding dress).
3. Most people cannot afford to buy a (cartier/Cartier) watch.
4. In most Indian villages, there is a (television/Television) set.
5. The parents gave the couple a (Sony/sony) television.
6. An American (refrigerator/Refrigerator) costs a lot of money in India.
7. The (Electrolux/electrolux) refrigerator is very popular.
8. Some women like to use expensive (handbags/Handbags).
9. Some women like (chanel/Chanel) handbags.
10. The couple wants to get a new (Washing machine/washing machine).

B. Answer the questions. Use correct capital letters.

1. What is your telephone's brand name? _____
2. What is your favorite brand name for clothes? _____
3. What is your favorite brand name for drinks? _____

UNIT 10

How Did Disneyland Start?

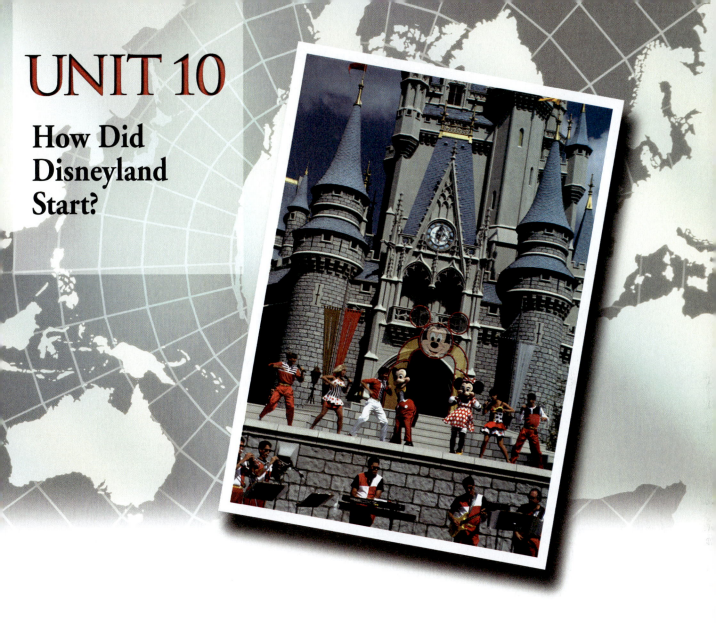

BEFORE YOU READ

Answer these questions.

1. What do you know about Disneyland?
2. Where is Disneyland?
3. What do you see in Disneyland?

How Did Disneyland Start?

1 One day, a man named Walt Disney took his daughters to an **amusement park**. At the amusement park, they went on the rides, played games, and saw animals. But the park was not **exciting**. It was also dirty. He **looked around** and said, "I want to take my children to a better place. I want families to **have fun** together."

2 Walt Disney was **famous for** his movies. He was also famous for his **cartoons**. Now Disney started to think about a new park. He wanted a park with different parts with special names. One part was "Fantasyland" and another part was "Adventureland." He also wanted to use **ideas** from his movies and cartoons. His most popular cartoon was Mickey Mouse. Disney wanted Mickey Mouse and other cartoon people to walk around the park and talk to the **guests**.

3 Disney's dream of a special park took many years to come true. People did not understand his ideas. Nobody wanted to give him money. So Disney used all his own money to build the park. On July 17, 1955, Disneyland opened in Anaheim, California. It was an **immediate** hit. The first year, about five million people went to Disneyland. People came from all over the United States and all over the world.

4 Walt Disney wanted Disneyland to be perfect. Every night, workers washed the streets. They **made sure** the streets were clean. They also made sure there was no chewing gum on the ground. They painted the **signs** again at night. They wanted the signs to look new.

5 Disneyland always had many plants and flowers. But Disney did not want any signs that said, "Do not walk on the plants." So every year, the workers changed 800,000 plants and put in new ones.

6 Disney wanted the workers to be happy and clean all the time. He started a special school for his workers called the University of Disneyland. The workers learned to be happy and **polite** to guests. They could not wear perfume, jewelry, or bright nail polish. They had to follow rules for how to dress and how to wear their hair.

7 Walt Disney became very rich. He was a millionaire. He died in 1966, but his dream of more Disneylands came true. In 1971, Walt Disney World opened in Orlando, Florida. Today, there are Disneylands in Tokyo and Paris.

VOCABULARY

MEANING

Write the correct words in the blanks.

cartoons	guests	amusement park	ideas
exciting	signs	polite	immediate

1. Disney took his daughters to an _____. They went on rides, played games, and saw animals.
2. Disney used different _____ for his park. He used information and things from other places.
3. Disney drew funny pictures of people and animals. He drew _____.
4. Disneyland has different _____. They have words and pictures on them.
5. The workers at Disneyland are _____. They are nice and respectful.
6. People were very happy to go to Disneyland. It was _____ to go.
7. Many people visit Disneyland, but they don't live there. They are _____.
8. Disneyland was an _____ hit. Everybody liked it right away.

WORDS THAT GO TOGETHER

Write the correct words in the blanks.

have fun	made sure	famous for	looked around

1. Disney saw different things at different places in the park. He _____ the park.
2. Disney wanted families to enjoy Disneyland. He wanted them to _____.
3. The workers checked that the streets were clean. They _____ they cleaned everything.
4. Everybody knows about Disney's movies. He is _____ his movies.

USE

Work with a partner to answer the questions. Use complete sentences.

1. When do you usually *have fun*?
2. What *signs* do you see on the street a lot?
3. What is an *exciting* place to go?
4. What is your favorite *cartoon*?
5. Who are you always *polite* to?
6. What do you like to do at an *amusement park*?

COMPREHENSION

UNDERSTANDING THE READING

Circle the letter of the correct answer.

1. Walt Disney's dream was _____.
   a. to open a special park   b. to open a park with movies   c. to draw Mickey Mouse cartoons

2. The workers at Disneyland _____.
   a. are happy and polite   b. clean every year   c. have signs

3. After Walt Disney died, _____.
   a. four million people went to Disneyland   b. other Disneylands opened   c. Disneyland moved

REMEMBERING DETAILS

Circle *T* if the sentence is true. Circle *F* if the sentence is false.

1.	People gave Disney money to start Disneyland.	T	F
2.	About five million people went to Disneyland in the first year.	T	F
3.	They changed the plants every week at Disneyland.	T	F
4.	Workers at Disneyland are always polite.	T	F
5.	There is a Disneyland in London.	T	F
6.	The first Disneyland opened in Orlando, Florida.	T	F

SENTENCE COMPLETION

Match the words in Column A and Column B to make sentences.

A

_____ 1. More Disneylands opened

_____ 2. Walt Disney wanted

_____ 3. The first Disneyland opened

_____ 4. People came

_____ 5. Workers wash

_____ 6. Disney's workers are

B

a. to open a special park.

b. in California.

c. in Tokyo and Paris.

d. happy and polite.

e. to Disneyland from all over America.

f. the streets of Disneyland every night.

DICTATION

Work with a partner. Read three sentences from the exercise above. Your partner listens and writes the sentences. Then your partner reads three sentences and you write them.

DISCUSSION

Discuss the answers to these questions with your classmates.

1. Disneyland started in the United States. Then Disneylands opened in other countries. What started in your country and then went to other countries?

2. What is another place where families have fun? What do they do there?

3. What is your favorite Walt Disney cartoon, book, or movie?

WRITING

Complete the sentences about Disneyland.

Example: Disneyland started in California. _____

1. Walt Disney was _____

2. Disneyland has _____

3. Walt Disney wanted _____

4. Disneyland workers _____

5. Other Disneylands _____

SPELLING AND PUNCTUATION

COMMAS: ADDRESSES AND DATES

We use a comma between the name of a city and the name of a state or country.

*Walt Disney World is in **Orlando, Florida.***

We use a comma between the number of the date and the number of the year.

*Disneyland opened on **July 17, 1955.***

We do <u>not</u> use a comma in a date with the name of the month and the number of the year.

*Disneyland opened in **July 1955.***

Put commas in the correct places. Three sentences do not need commas.

1. Walt Disney was born in December 1901.
2. Walt Disney was born on December 5 1901.
3. Mickey Mouse became a star in May 1928.
4. Disneyland opened on July 17 1955.
5. Disneyland is in Anaheim California.
6. Disney died on December 15 1966.
7. Disney died in Hollywood California.
8. There is a Disneyland in Tokyo.
9. Paris France has a Disneyland, too.
10. Disneyland Paris opened on April 12 1992.

SELF-TEST 1
Units 1–10

A. SENTENCE COMPLETION

Circle the letter of the correct answer.

1. J.K. Rowling _____.
   a. writing two more books   c. wrote more two books
   b. write two more books   d. wrote two more books

2. Chinese New Year _____.
   a. is a holiday special   c. is special holiday
   b. is a special holiday   d. special holiday

3. Buckingham Palace _____.
   a. there are about 600 rooms   c. has about 600 rooms
   b. it has about 600 rooms   d. have about 600 rooms

4. The most important animal in India _____.
   a. is the cow   c. are the cow
   b. is the cows   d. is cows

5. At the end of October, Mexicans prepare _____.
   a. celebrate the Day of the Dead   c. celebrated the Day of the Dead
   b. to celebrate the Day of the Dead   d. celebrating the Day of the Dead

6. Today the Inuit's lives are very different. They _____ from stores.
   a. bought food and clothes   c. buy food and clothes
   b. by food and clothes   d. buys food and clothes

7. The Beatles _____.
   a. was from England   c. to be from England
   b. were from England   d. is from England

8. The Chinese _____ thousands of years ago.
   a. built the Great Wall   c. build the Great Wall
   b. building the Great Wall   d. to build the Great Wall

9. People _____ for weddings.
   a. gifts give   c. giving gifts
   b. give gifts   d. gives gifts

10. Walt Disney _____ very rich.
   a. he was   c. became
   b. were   d. be

B. VOCABULARY

Complete the definitions. Circle the letter of the correct answer.

1. She wrote a book. She is the _____.
   a. adult   b. author   c. guest   d. foreigner

2. You are interested in the Chinese beliefs and way of life. You are
   interested in Chinese _____.
   a. interview   b. signs   c. reasons   d. culture

3. You want many of something. You want _____ it.
   a. on top of   b. the same as   c. a lot of   d. a little of

4. You want something to look nice. You _____ it.
   a. cost   b. eat   c. use   d. decorate

5. You want to dry your hands. You use _____.
   a. a candle   b. skins   c. a towel   d. a flag

6. You always write letters to people and call them. You _____ them.
   a. break up   b. keep in touch with   c. have a picnic   d. tell stories

7. Some people like a famous person very much. They are _____ of
   the famous person.
   a. politicians   b. authors   c. fans   d. concerts

8. You want to keep something safe. You don't want bad things to happen to it. You _____ it.
   a. protect   b. practice   c. remember   d. pull

9. You have enough money to buy something. You can _____ it.
   a. prepare   b. hit   c. afford   d. sell

10. You are nice to people. You show respect to people. You are _____.
    a. polite   b. modern   c. exciting   d. bright

C. SPELLING AND PUNCTUATION

Circle the letter of the sentence with the correct spelling and punctuation.

1. a. J.K. Rowling wrote *harry Potter*.
   b. J.K. Rowling wrote *Harry Potter*.
   c. J.k. Rowling wrote *Harry Potter*.
   d. J.K. Rowling wrote *harry potter*.

2. a. People celebrate New year's day around the world.
   b. People celebrate New year's Day around the world.
   c. People celebrate New Year's Day around the world.
   d. People celebrate New Year's day around the world.

3. a. Queen elizabeth lives in Buckingham Palace.
   b. Qween Elizabeth lives in Buckingham Palace.
   c. Queen Elizabeth lives in Buckingham Palace.
   d. Quween Elizabeth lives in Buckingham Palace.

4. a. The farms arn't busy at certain times.
   b. The farms are'nt busy at certain times.
   c. The farms aren't busy at certain times.
   d. The farms are'not busy at certain times.

5. a. They eat, drink, play music, and sing.
   b. They eat drink, play music, and sing.
   c. They eat, drink play music, and sing.
   d. They eat, drink, play music, and, sing.

6. a. The Inuit live in very cold countrys.
   b. The Inuit live in very cold countries.
   c. The inuit live in very cold countries.
   d. The Inuit live in very cold countryes.

7. a. John and Paul were writeing many songs.
   b. John and paul were writeing many songs.
   c. John, and Paul were writing many songs.
   d. John and Paul were writing many songs.

8. a. The Great Wall is a Structure in China.
   b. The Great wall is a structure in China.
   c. The Great Wall is a structure in China.
   d. The great wall is a structure in China.

9. a. They like Singer Sewing Machines in India.
   b. They like Singer sewing machines in India.
   c. They like singer sewing machines in India.
   d. They like Singer Sewing machines in India.

10. a. Disneyland is in Anaheim California.
    b. Disneyland is in, Anaheim, California.
    c. Disneyland is in anaheim, California.
    d. Disneyland is in Anaheim, California.

UNIT 11

Who Is Andrew Carnegie?

BEFORE YOU READ

Answer these questions.

1. Andrew Carnegie was very rich. What do you know about rich people?
2. How do people become rich?
3. What do rich people do with their money?

Who Is Andrew Carnegie?

1 Andrew Carnegie was born in 1835 in Scotland. He was from a poor family. When he was twelve, his family moved to the United States. They wanted a better life.

2 The Carnegie family lived in Pittsburgh, Pennsylvania. Andrew started to work **right away**. He got a job in a **factory**. He was a good worker, but he didn't like the job. Later, he changed his job. He worked at the Pennsylvania Railroad Company. Everybody there liked Andrew. He did many different jobs. His salary got higher every year.

3 In his free time, Andrew loved to read. He lived near Colonel James Anderson. Colonel Anderson was a rich man with many books. He **let** young boys use his library for free. In those days, the United States did not have free public libraries. Andrew read **as much as possible**. He read **throughout** his life. He always thought that reading was very important.

4 Andrew learned a lot at the railroad company. He **realized** that the railroad was very important for big countries. He had an idea to start a business with railroads. He **saved** all his money and opened a business. He was thirty years old.

5 First, his company made **bridges** for the railroads. Ten years later, they made steel. The Carnegie Steel Company became the largest company in the United States. They made steel for bridges, machines, and many other things. People called Carnegie the "Steel King." Soon he was the richest man in the world.

6 Carnegie liked to make money. But he believed it was very important to help other people. In 1901, he sold his company for $480 million. He started to **give away** his money to make new libraries and colleges all over the United States. He built 2,811 libraries. Carnegie also gave a lot of money to people who worked for **peace**. In 1903, he gave $1.5 million to build a Peace Palace in the Netherlands.

7 Andrew Carnegie died in 1919. He was eighty-four years old. During his life, he gave away **nearly** all of his money. He gave away over $350 million for education and peace. There are colleges, libraries, hospitals, and parks **named after** Andrew Carnegie. He has helped millions of people all over the world to study and learn.

VOCABULARY

MEANING

Write the correct words in the blanks.

throughout	factory	let	nearly
peace	saved	bridges	realized

1. Andrew worked in a building where people make things. He worked in a
   _____.

2. Andrew read from the beginning to the end of his life. He read
   _____ his life.

3. Andrew _____ that the railroad was important. He knew and
   understood that this was true.

4. The trains on the railroad needed to go over rivers and roads. Carnegie
   made _____ for the railroad.

5. Carnegie did not want war or fighting. He wanted _____.

6. Carnegie kept his money to use later. He _____ his money.

7. Colonel Anderson wanted the boys to use his library. He allowed them to
   read the books. He _____ them use the library.

8. Carnegie gave almost all of his money for education and peace. He gave
   away _____ all his money.

WORDS THAT GO TOGETHER

Write the correct words in the blanks.

named after	as much as possible
give away	right away

1. Andrew started to work immediately. He worked _____.

2. Carnegie wanted other people to have his money. He wanted to
   _____ his money.

3. The Carnegie Library is in Pittsburgh. It is _____
   Andrew Carnegie.

4. Carnegie was busy at the factory. Sometimes he had free time. He read in
   his free time. He read _____.

USE

Work with a partner to answer the questions. Use complete sentences.

1. What is something you *saved* this year?
2. What do you do *right away* after school or work?
3. What do you do *throughout* your school life?
4. What is the name of a famous *bridge*?
5. What is made in a *factory*?
6. What building is *named* after someone famous?

COMPREHENSION

UNDERSTANDING THE READING

Circle the letter of the correct answer.

1. Andrew Carnegie opened his own _____.
   a. bridge   b. steel company   c. railroad

2. Andrew and the boys went to _____.
   a. the factory   b. the public library   c. Colonel Anderson's library

3. Carnegie became the richest man in _____.
   a. Pittsburgh   b. the United States   c. the world

REMEMBERING DETAILS

Reread the passage and answer the questions.

1. Where was Andrew Carnegie born?
2. When did he start to work?
3. What did his first company make?
4. What did he make steel for?
5. When did he sell his company?
6. How many libraries did he build?

UNDERSTANDING THE SEQUENCE

Which happened first? Write *1* on the line. Which happened second? Write *2* on the line.

1. _____ Carnegie worked at the Pennsylvania Railroad Company.

    _____ Carnegie worked in a factory.

2. _____ Carnegie made bridges for railroads.

    _____ Carnegie made steel.

3. _____ Carnegie became the richest man in the world.

    _____ People called Carnegie the "Steel King."

4. _____ Carnegie built libraries and colleges.

    _____ Carnegie sold his company.

TELL THE STORY

Work with a partner. Tell the story of Andrew Carnegie to your partner. Use your own words. Your partner asks you questions about the story. Then your partner tells you the story and you ask questions.

DISCUSSION

Discuss the answers to these questions with your classmates.

1. Imagine you are the richest person in the world. What would you do with your money?
2. Does money always make people happy? Explain.
3. Carnegie's family was poor. Later, he made a lot of money. Do you know anyone like this? Tell their story.

WRITING

Complete the sentences about Andrew Carnegie.

Example: Carnegie was born in Scotland. _____

1. Carnegie worked _____

2. Carnegie loved _____

3. Carnegie started _____

4. Carnegie became _____

5. Carnegie gave _____

SPELLING AND PUNCTUATION

 NUMBERS AS WORDS

The words *hundred, thousand,* and *million* are plural when there are no numbers before them.

*He gave away **millions** of dollars.*
*There are **hundreds** of people here.*

When there is a number before them, they are singular.

*He gave away over $350 **million**.*
*There are five **hundred** people here.*

We use a hyphen (–) between two-word numbers from *twenty-one* to *ninety-nine*.

eighty–four   thirty–one

Write *C* for numbers with correct spelling and punctuation. Rewrite numbers with incorrect spelling or punctuation.

1. ninety one   _____
2. thir-teen   _____
3. fiftytwo   _____
4. thirty-five   _____
5. million of people   _____
6. two thousands   _____
7. twelve hundred   _____
8. three millions   _____
9. four hundreds dollars _____
10. twenty nine   _____

UNIT 12

What Is Life Like in Antarctica?

BEFORE YOU READ

Answer these questions.

1. What do you see in the picture?
2. Do you think the people live there?
3. Do you think it is beautiful?

What Is Life Like in Antarctica?

1 Antarctica is like no other place in the world. It is **unique**. It is very big. It is like the United States and Australia together. Antarctica is the coldest place in the world. The **temperature** is sometimes –125°F (–87°C). August and September are the coldest months because there is no sun.

2 Antarctica is at the southern tip of the world. It is the highest **continent**. It is 10,000 feet high. Antarctica also has very strong winds. The wind sometimes **blows** two hundred miles an hour. It is also the driest place in the world. Antarctica is drier than the Sahara Desert!

3 Antarctica is also **empty**. There are **huge** glaciers and ice everywhere. A glacier is an area of ice that moves slowly. The ice and glaciers are beautiful. But most plants and land animals cannot live on the ice. It is too cold. There are no trees, no rivers, and no cities in Antarctica. There are no land animals. Only penguins and other sea birds live there.

4 Antarctica does not **belong to** any one country. In fact, every country owns Antarctica. More than twenty countries have stations in Antarctica. A station is a place where scientists do **experiments**. There are **separate** stations for different countries. The scientists are the only people who live in Antarctica. **In all**, over four thousand people live at the stations in the summer. Over one thousand people live there in the winter.

5 Life on an Antarctica station is hard. It is like life on a space station. The sun shines for six months, and then it is night for six months. People usually have problems with sleeping and eating. They eat more because they are not busy. In an emergency, it is hard to get help. In 1999, an American doctor named Jerri Nielsen realized she was sick. She had cancer. It was winter, and airplanes could not land in Antarctica. She was the only doctor there. Dr. Nielsen **had no choice**. She had to stay. An airplane **dropped** medicine to her, and she took care of herself. Several months later, Dr. Nielsen returned to the United States to get special medical help.

6 Today, more and more people visit Antarctica. Ships go to Antarctica during the summer months from November to February. People want to visit this unusual place, but they don't want to live there!

VOCABULARY

MEANING

Write the correct words in the blanks.

continent	temperature	blows	dropped	unique
empty	huge	experiments	separate	

1. The medicine fell from the plane. It _____ from the plane.

2. It is very cold in Antarctica. The _____ is sometimes –125°F (–87°C).

3. The wind _____ two hundred miles an hour. The winds move very fast.

4. There is nothing in Antarctica. It is _____.

5. The glaciers are very, very big. They are _____.

6. Scientists go to Antarctica to do special tests. They do _____.

7. Antarctica is different from the other continents. It is special. Antarctica is _____.

8. The stations are not joined together. They are _____ from each other.

9. The United States is a large country. It is on the _____ of North America.

WORDS THAT GO TOGETHER

Write the correct words in the blanks.

belong to	had no choice	in all

1. There were a total of four thousand people there. There were four thousand people _____.

2. Who owns Antarctica? Who does Antarctica _____?

3. Dr. Nielsen could not do something else. She _____.

USE

Work with a partner to answer the questions. Use complete sentences.

1. What are the seven *continents*?
2. What is the *temperature* today?
3. How many people are in your family *in all*?
4. What science *experiment* is interesting?
5. When does the wind *blow* a lot?
6. What movie was a *huge* hit this year?

COMPREHENSION

UNDERSTANDING THE READING

Circle the letter of the correct answer.

1. Antarctica belongs to _____.
    a. the United States   b. every country   c. twenty countries

2. Scientists live in Antarctica _____.
    a. in the summer   b. in the winter   c. in the summer and the winter

3. On an Antarctic station _____.
    a. people eat less   b. there is no space   c. life is difficult

REMEMBERING DETAILS

Circle *T* if the sentence is true. Circle *F* if the sentence is false.

1. Antarctica is drier than the Sahara Desert.   T   F
2. The wind blows three hundred miles an hour.   T   F
3. Most plants and animals can live on the ice.   T   F
4. People have problems sleeping in Antarctica.   T   F
5. People visit Antarctica in July and August.   T   F
6. Penguins live in Antarctica.   T   F

SENTENCE COMPLETION

Match the words in Column A and Column B to make sentences.

A

_____ 1. Scientists live

_____ 2. Antarctica has

_____ 3. Antarctica is

_____ 4. The sun shines

_____ 5. Scientists do

_____ 6. Antarctica doesn't belong

B

a. the coldest place in the world.

b. on stations in Antarctica.

c. very strong winds.

d. experiments in Antarctica.

e. to one country.

f. for six months of the year.

DICTATION

Work with a partner. Read three sentences from the exercise above. Your partner listens and writes the sentences. Then your partner reads three sentences and you write them.

DISCUSSION

Discuss the answers to these questions with your classmates.

1. Do you want to visit Antarctica? Why or why not?
2. Antarctica is an unusual place to visit. What are other unusual places to visit?
3. What do you think scientists find in Antarctica?

WRITING

Complete the sentences about Antarctica.

Example: Antarctica is _a continent._ _____

1. Antarctica is _____
2. Antarctica has _____
3. There are _____
4. Scientists _____
5. People _____

SPELLING AND PUNCTUATION

MONTHS IN THE YEAR

There are twelve months in the year. Usually, we write the complete name.

August and *September* are the coldest months.

Here are the names of the twelve months of the year.

January	April	July	October
February	May	August	November
March	June	September	December

Sometimes we shorten, or *abbreviate*, the names of the months. We often abbreviate on forms or checks. We put a period after the abbreviation.

A. Circle the correct abbreviation. You may use a dictionary.

1. **January**	Janu.	Jan.	Jany
2. **February**	Febr.	Feby	Feb.
3. **March**	Mar.	Mch.	Mach.
4. **April**	Al.	Apr.	Ap.
5. **May**	My	May.	no abbreviation
6. **June**	Jne.	Jun.	no abbreviation
7. **July**	Jul.	Jly	no abbreviation
8. **August**	Aug.	Ast.	Ag.
9. **September**	Sep.	Sept.	Spt.
10. **October**	Octo.	Oct.	Oc.
11. **November**	Nbr.	Nov.	Nr.
12. **December**	Der.	Decb.	Dec.

Most months have thirty days or thirty-one days. February is special; it usually has twenty-eight days. Every four years is a leap year. In a leap year, February has twenty-nine days. This is a poem children learn in school to remember how many days each month has.

Thirty days has September / April, June, and November. / All the rest have thirty-one, / Except February, which has twenty-eight. / In a leap year, twenty-nine.

B. Answer the questions.

1. Which months have thirty days? _____

2. Which months have thirty-one days? _____

3. Which month usually has twenty-eight days? _____

UNIT 13

Where Do People Live Under the Ground?

Answer these questions.

1. What can you say about the man in the picture?
2. Why do you think he is under the ground?
3. Do you know other places in the world where people live under the ground?

Where Do People Live Under the Ground?

1 One place where people live under the ground is a small town called Coober Pedy. Coober Pedy is in the Outback of south Australia. Most of the people in Coober Pedy are miners. Miners **dig** under the ground. They **look for** gold or special stones. Coober Pedy is famous for opals. Opals are beautiful white stones. People put opals in jewelry.

2 Miners **discovered** opals in Coober Pedy in 1915. At that time, many miners lived in simple **holes** under the ground. Aboriginal people laughed at them. The Aboriginal people are the **native** people of Australia. They called the area *kupa piti*. This means "white man in a hole" in their language.

3 Today, the homes are not simple holes. About four thousand people live in Coober Pedy. About half the people live under the ground. Coober Pedy has homes, restaurants, hotels, and churches. It is like other towns. But the people don't have a **view**. A new underground house with five rooms costs about $25,000. Some homes have swimming pools!

4 The people of Coober Pedy live underground for different reasons. One reason is there are no trees. The last tree died in 1971. People need wood from trees to build houses. The **main** reason why people live underground is the very hot weather. The temperature in the summer goes up to 122° F [50° C]. Underground, the temperature is 77° F [25° C].

5 People also live under the ground in the Sahara Desert in south Tunisia. It is very hot and there are no trees. The people there are called Berbers. The Berbers dig **deep** holes in the ground. Many houses have two or three floors, but they are simple. Air and light come through an open hole. There are about seven hundred of these holes.

6 Thousands of years ago, people hid underground in Cappadocia, Turkey. People still live there today. It is a beautiful place with good weather. **In the future**, more people will live under the ground. They will have different reasons. Japan has a lot of people and little land. Japan wants to build a city under the ground. The name of the city will be Alice City. About 100,000 people will live there. It will have offices, hotels, sports centers, and theaters.

7 Underground cities are very interesting, **of course**. But can people live with no sun and no sky?

VOCABULARY

MEANING

Write the correct words in the blanks.

dig	discovered	deep	native
holes	view	main	

1. Miners make holes in the ground around Coober Pedy. They _____ in the ground.

2. The Berbers live far down in the ground. They live _____ in the ground.

3. In 1915, miners _____ opals in Coober Pedy. They found opals there.

4. The Aborigines were born in Australia. They are the _____ people.

5. There are many reasons why people live underground. The weather is the most important reason. It is the _____ reason.

6. The people underground can't see other things outside. They do not have a _____.

7. The people live in openings in the ground. They live in _____.

WORDS THAT GO TOGETHER

Write the correct words in the blanks.

look for	in the future	of course

1. More people will live underground at a later time. They will live underground _____.

2. Miners try to find many things underground. They _____ gold or special stones.

3. I am not surprised that people like to live underground. It is an interesting place to live. _____, people like to live there.

USE

Work with a partner to answer the questions. Use complete sentences.

1. What animal likes to *dig*?
2. What is the *main* reason you want to learn English?
3. What is the *view* from a window in your home?
4. What are some reasons people dig *holes*?
5. Why do people go in *deep* water?
6. What do you want to do *in the future*?

COMPREHENSION

UNDERSTANDING THE READING

Circle the letter of the correct answer.

1. People in Coober Pedy live under the ground because _____.
   a. it costs $25,000   b. they have trees   c. it is not hot there

2. There are about seven hundred holes with homes around them in _____.
   a. Japan   b. Tunisia   c. Coober Pedy

3. Japan is planning an underground city because _____.
   a. they have a lot of people   b. they have a lot of land   c. it is very hot

REMEMBERING DETAILS

Reread the passage and answer the questions.

1. Where is Coober Pedy?
2. How many people live in Coober Pedy?
3. What are the native people of Australia called?
4. What did the miners discover in 1915?
5. How many holes are there in the Sahara Desert?
6. What is the name of the city Japan is planning to build?

SENTENCE COMPLETION

Match the words in Column A and Column B to make sentences.

A	B
____ 1. Coober Pedy is	a. two or three floors.
____ 2. Japan has	b. very hot above the ground.
____ 3. The Berber houses have	c. homes and restaurants.
____ 4. Coober Pedy has	d. little land.
____ 5. Underground homes don't have	e. under the ground for valuable things.
____ 6. Miners dig	f. a view

DICTATION

Work with a partner. Read three sentences from the exercise above. Your partner listens and writes the sentences. Then your partner reads three sentences and you write them.

DISCUSSION

Discuss the answers to these questions with your classmates.

1. Would you like to live underground? What would be the best thing? What would be the worst thing?
2. What do you think about Japan's underground city?
3. Where are some other unusual places people live?

WRITING

Complete the sentences about people who live under the ground.

Example: People live under the ground _in Coober Pedy._____

1. Miners dig _____
2. Coober Pedy has _____
3. One reason people live underground _____
4. Another place people live underground _____
5. In the future, _____

SPELLING AND PUNCTUATION

 EXCLAMATION POINTS

> We use an exclamation point at the end of a sentence to show strong emotion (feeling or excitement) or a strong command. An exclamation point makes the words stronger and louder.
>
> *Some homes have swimming pools!*
> *Ken! Come here!*
>
> We do **not** use a period before or after an exclamation point.

A. Write *C* for sentences with correct punctuation. Rewrite the incorrect sentences. Use exclamation points. Use periods for incorrect exclamation points.

1. Look. There's a man in the hole.

   _____

2. The native people of Australia are called Aborigines.

   _____

3. What a great idea.

   _____

4. Wow. There are no trees in the town.

   _____

5. Coober Pedy is a town in the south of Australia!.

   _____

6. Miners work under the ground.

   _____

7. The miners found thousands of opals!.

   _____

B. Write two sentences with exclamation points.

   _____

   _____

UNIT 14

Why Do People Decorate Their Bodies?

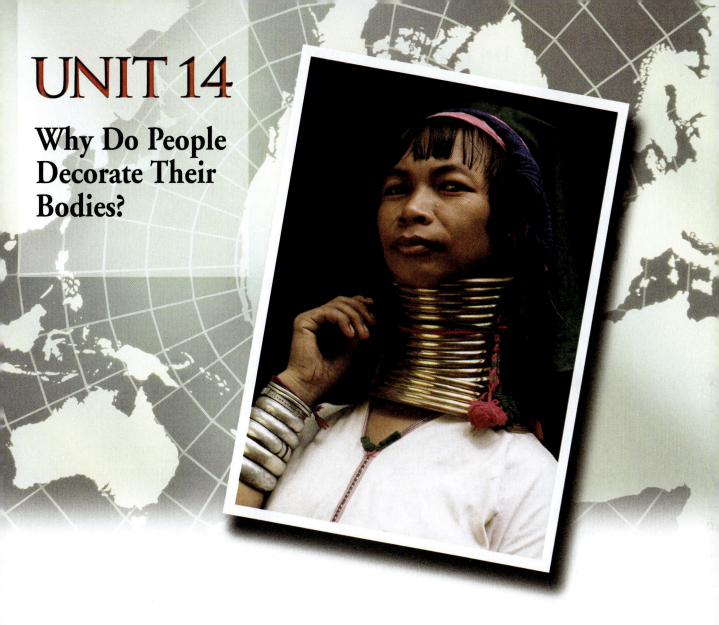

BEFORE YOU READ

Answer these questions.

1. What body decorations do women wear?
2. What body decorations do men wear?
3. What body decorations do you like?

Why Do People Decorate Their Bodies?

1 People decorate their bodies for many reasons. They also decorate in different ways. Some groups of people have decorated their bodies for thousands of years. Other people want to look **attractive**. Other people want to **belong to** a group.

2 Some people decorate their **lips**, ears, and neck to be beautiful. For example, in Africa, the Surmese women wear a plate in their bottom lip. How do they do this? First, a mother makes a hole in her daughter's bottom lip. Then she **stretches** the lip. Then she **puts** a small plate **in** it. As the daughter gets older, she puts in bigger and bigger plates. Other people in Africa put plates in their ears. They want the bottom of their ears to hang to their shoulders.

3 The Pa Daung women in Myanmar are called "giraffe women." They have very long necks, like giraffes. The women wear metal rings to stretch their necks. They wear more rings as they get older. Their necks become longer. Their necks are sometimes two or three times the **normal** size. Some women die if they **take off** the rings.

4 People also decorate their teeth to be beautiful. Many Americans and Europeans like white, **straight** teeth. They spend a lot of money to fix and clean their teeth. This is not true in other parts of the world. In east Africa, some people **pull out** their bottom teeth. They want their top teeth to **stick out**. In some parts of Asia, women used to paint their teeth black to look beautiful. Today, young people do not do this. In Indonesia, boys and girls file their teeth. A person with filed teeth will have a good and healthy life.

5 People around the world always liked tattoos. Europeans learned about tattoos around 1770. A famous English explorer named Captain Cook went to Tahiti. He saw people there with tattoos. The Tahitians called the decoration *tatou*. From this, we get the word *tattoo*. The Tahitians taught Cook and his sailors how to make tattoos. The sailors **returned** to England, and other people liked their tattoos. Soon tattoos **spread** to the rest of Europe. Many sailors still have tattoos.

6 Today, many different types of people have tattoos. For some people, body decorations are attractive. For other people, they are strange.

VOCABULARY

MEANING

Write the correct words in the blanks.

| attractive | normal | returned | straight |
| lips | stretches | spread | |

1. The women's necks are longer than the usual size. They are longer than the _____ size.

2. In Africa, a group of women like plates in their _____. The plate is on the outside edge of the mouth.

3. Some women decorate their bodies to be beautiful. They want to be _____.

4. The sailors went back to their home. They _____ home.

5. Her teeth are _____. They do not bend or curve. They are like a line.

6. The mother pulls her daughter's lip. She wants the lip to be bigger and longer. She _____ it.

7. People all over Europe learned about tattoos. Tattoos _____ from England to Europe.

WORDS THAT GO TOGETHER

Write the correct words in the blanks.

| pull out | belong to | puts in | stick out | take off |

1. Many people want to _____ a group. They want to be together with other people.

2. Their teeth come out far from their face. The teeth _____.

3. Why do some people remove their teeth? Why do they _____ their teeth?

4. The woman adds a small plate to her lip. She _____ a plate.

5. The woman is wearing neck rings. She wants to remove them. She will _____ the rings.

USE

Work with a partner to answer the questions. Use complete sentences.

1. What do many women put on their *lips*?
2. What part of your body do you *stretch*?
3. What time do you *return* home after school or work?
4. What kind of food is in a *normal* breakfast for you?
5. What group do you *belong to*?
6. What body decoration looks *attractive* on many people?

COMPREHENSION

UNDERSTANDING THE READING

Circle the letter of the correct answer.

1. In Africa, they decorate their lips and ears to show they are _____.
   a. old   b. beautiful   c. rich

2. Sailors learned about tattoos in _____.
   a. England   b. Europe   c. Tahiti

3. Today, many different people _____.
   a. want black teeth   b. have tattoos   c. go to Tahiti

REMEMBERING DETAILS

Reread the passage and answer the questions.

1. What do some women in Africa put in their earlobes?
2. Why are the Pa Daung women called "giraffe women"?
3. Where do some people pull out their bottom teeth?
4. What color did some women paint their teeth in Asia?
5. Who was Captain Cook?
6. Where did Captain Cook see tattoos?

SENTENCE COMPLETION

Match the words in Column A and Column B to make sentences.

A

____ 1. Many Americans and Europeans like

____ 2. Some women in Myanmar stretch

____ 3. Some women in Asia painted

____ 4. People decorate

____ 5. Some young people have tattoos to

____ 6. Tattoos spread to

B

a. their teeth black.

b. their bodies for many reasons.

c. belong to a group.

d. white teeth.

e. the rest of Europe.

f. their necks.

DICTATION

Work with a partner. Read three sentences from the exercise above. Your partner listens and writes the sentences. Then your partner reads three sentences and you write them.

DISCUSSION

Discuss the answers to these questions with your classmates.

1. What body decoration is popular in your country?
2. What body decoration do you want to have?
3. What are other ways to decorate the body?

WRITING

Complete the sentences about body decoration.

Example: People decorate their bodies *to be attractive.* _____

1. In Africa, some women _____
2. In Myanmar, some women _____
3. In Asia, some women _____
4. In east Africa, some people _____
5. Some people get tattoos _____

Why Do People Decorate Their Bodies?   87

SPELLING AND PUNCTUATION

 PLURALS: NOUNS ENDING IN *–O*

> **Some singular nouns end in –o. Look at the letter before the –o.**
>
> If the letter is a vowel, add **–s**.
> *tattoo—tattoos*   *radio—radios*
>
> If the letter is a consonant, add **–es**.
> *echo—echoes*
>
> **Some words have special rules.**
> *piano—pianos*   *solo—solos*   *kilo—kilos*   *halo—halos*

A. Circle the correctly spelled word in each group. You may use a dictionary.

1. potatoes   potatos
2. radioes   radios

3. patios   patioes
4. rodeos   rodeoes

B. Underline the misspelled words. Write the correct words on the lines.

1. His hair is very red. It looks like tomatos.   _____

2. He probably uses special shampooes.   _____

3. The lead singer of the group has tattooes.   _____

4. He likes to sing soloes.   _____

5. The group has many videoes.   _____

6. The group goes to different studioes to record.   _____

7. They put on kiloes of makeup.   _____

8. They bring their own pianoes with them.   _____

9. I love their songs. The songs have echos.   _____

10. They have crazy hair, but they are my heros.   _____

UNIT 15

How Did the Red Cross Start?

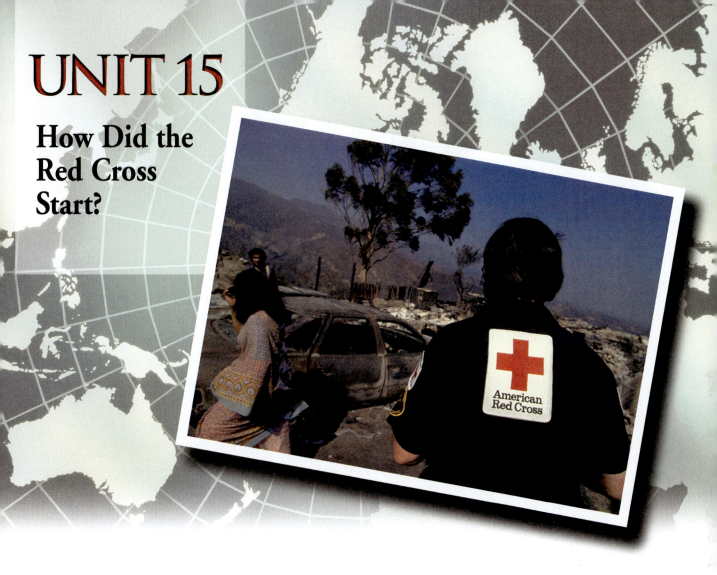

BEFORE YOU READ

Answer these questions.

1. What do you know about the Red Cross?
2. What do you know about the sign of the Red Cross?
3. Who does the Red Cross help?

How Did the Red Cross Start?

1 In 1859, a Swiss man named Henry Dunant went to Italy. He went there **on business**. There was a war in the town of Solferino. Dunant saw the war, and he was **shocked**. There were thousands of **wounded** men. Nobody was there to take care of them.

2 Dunant asked the people in the town to help the wounded men. Later, he wrote a book called *A Memory of Solferino*. He had a good idea to help people in wars. He wanted every country to have **volunteers**. The volunteers take care of the wounded people in wars.

3 In 1863, Dunant and four other Swiss men started the Red Cross. A year later, twelve countries **signed** a paper in Geneva, Switzerland. Dunant traveled to other countries. He wanted to make the Red Cross bigger and better all over the world.

4 **By now**, Dunant was famous. But his own business had problems. His business had no money. Some people in Geneva were angry because they **lost money**, too. Dunant **resigned** from the Red Cross. Now he had no money and no home. He slept in the streets and had nothing to eat. For twenty years, he lived on different streets in Switzerland. In 1890, a teacher found him in a Swiss village. The teacher told everybody that Dunant was alive. But nobody cared.

5 Dunant became very sick. He went to a hospital for the poor in the town of Heiden. Dunant stayed in the same room for eighteen years. It was Room 12. In 1895, a **journalist** found him and wrote about him. Then Dunant became famous again. People gave him prizes and money. But Dunant stayed in Room 12.

6 Dunant died in 1910. There was no funeral ceremony. He wanted everything to be simple. Dunant gave his money to the hospital workers. He also gave money for a "free bed" in the hospital. This "free bed" was for the poor sick people of Heiden.

7 The **symbol** of the Red Cross is a red cross on a white flag. It is the **reverse** of the flag of Switzerland. Muslim countries have a red crescent. A crescent looks like a half-moon. Today, more than 170 countries are part of the Red Cross and Red Crescent. The volunteers help people in many ways. Everybody remembers Henry Dunant and his good idea.

VOCABULARY

MEANING

Write the correct words in the blanks.

shocked	wounded	volunteers	reverse
resigned	signed	symbol	journalist

1. He writes stories for newspapers and magazines. He is a

   _____.

2. Many soldiers were _____. They were badly hurt.

3. People took care of the wounded men. They did not get paid money.
   They were _____.

4. People from twelve countries _____ a paper. They added their
   names to the paper.

5. Dunant stopped working at the Red Cross. He _____ from
   his job.

6. A red cross on a white background is the _____ of the Red
   Cross. It is the Red Cross's sign.

7. Dunant was very surprised and upset. He was _____.

8. The Swiss flag has a white cross and a red flag. The Red Cross flag has
   a red cross and a white flag. The Swiss flag is the _____ of the
   Red Cross flag.

WORDS THAT GO TOGETHER

Write the correct words in the blanks.

on business	lost money	by now

1. Dunant did not go to the town of Solferino for a vacation. He went

   _____.

2. Dunant had a lot of money before and up until this time. He was rich

   _____.

3. Dunant's business was very good. Then the business had problems.
   The owners of the business _____.

USE

Work with a partner to answer these questions. Use complete sentences.

1. What *shocks* you?
2. Who is a famous *journalist*?
3. How do *volunteers* help people?
4. What is something you *sign*?
5. What is something people do *on business*?
6. Why does a person usually *resign* from a job?

COMPREHENSION

UNDERSTANDING THE READING

Circle the letter of the correct answer.

1. Dunant asked the people of Solferino to _____.
   a. help wounded men   b. end the war   c. join the Red Cross

2. Henry Dunant _____.
   a. always worked for   b. became poor and   c. was sick all his life
      the Red Cross   alone

3. The symbol of the Red Cross is _____.
   a. different in every   b. the same in every   c. a red cross or red
      country   country   crescent

REMEMBERING DETAILS

Reread the passage and answer the questions.

1. What country did Henry Dunant go to in 1859?
2. What shocked Dunant?
3. What was Dunant's idea?
4. Where did twelve countries sign the paper for the Red Cross?
5. Where did Dunant stay for eighteen years?
6. How many countries are part of the Red Cross and Red Crescent today?

UNDERSTANDING THE SEQUENCE

Which happened first? Write *1* on the line. Which happened second? Write *2* on the line.

1. _____ Dunant wrote a book.

   _____ Dunant was shocked at the town of Solferino.

2. _____ Dunant and four other men started the Red Cross.

   _____ Twelve countries signed a paper in Geneva.

3. _____ Dunant became very sick.

   _____ Dunant lived alone on different streets.

4. _____ Dunant received money and prizes.

   _____ A journalist wrote about Dunant.

TELL THE STORY

Work with a partner. Tell the story of Henry Dunant to your partner. Use your own words. Your partner asks you questions about the story. Then your partner tells you the story and you ask questions.

DISCUSSION

Discuss the answers to these questions with your classmates.

1. The Red Cross is an international group. They help people all over the world. What other international groups do you know? What do they do?

2. Is it better to give money to a group or help in another way?

3. Do you want to belong to a group that helps people? How do you want to help?

WRITING

Complete the sentences about the Red Cross.

Example: The Red Cross started in Switzerland._____

1. Henry Dunant went _____

2. Henry Dunant had an idea _____

3. Henry Dunant and four other Swiss men _____

4. Henry Dunant gave money_____

5. The Red Cross is_____

SPELLING AND PUNCTUATION

CAPITAL LETTERS: ORGANIZATIONS AND RELIGIONS

We use a capital letter for the main words in the name of an organization.
We do <u>not</u> use a capital letter for *the* or *of* in the name.

*The symbol of the **R**ed **C**ross is a red cross on a white flag.*

We use a capital letter for the names of religions and their followers.

*Many **M**uslims help the poor in different countries.*

Underline the words that need capital letters. Circle the words with incorrect capital letters.

1. The red cross is an Organization.
2. The Symbol of the red cross is a red cross on a white flag.
3. The red crescent has offices in muslim countries.
4. The red cross takes care of people from all religions—christians, hindus, muslims, and jews.
5. Another Organization that helps people is doctors without borders.
6. The Organization oxfam started in 1971.
7. Many Organizations help poor and sick hindu, buddhist, christian, and muslim children in Africa.
8. There are a lot of roman catholics in Switzerland.
9. The protestants are the second largest religious group in Switzerland.
10. There are about 150,000 muslims in Switzerland.

UNIT 16

Who Are the Blue Men of the Sahara?

BEFORE YOU READ

Answer these questions.

1. Where is the Sahara?
2. Who lives in the Sahara?
3. Why do you think the men of the Sahara are "blue"?

Who Are the Blue Men of the Sahara?

1 The Blue Men of the Sahara is a name for the Tuareg people. People call them this name because they wear blue clothes. There are between 300,000 and one million Tuareg today. They have lived in the Sahara Desert for thousands of years. It is hot, dry, and windy there. Their lives are difficult because of the desert weather and life.

2 The Tuareg do not live in one place. They move from **place to place** to find water and food for their animals. The Tuareg live in groups of four or five families. Everybody helps each other. The men take care of the animals. The women **put up** the tents. The Tuareg live and sleep in the tents. Tuareg tents are usually **made of** animal skins, but today some Tuareg have plastic tents.

3 The Tuareg dress in a special way. The men **cover** their faces. The women do not. The men travel a lot in the desert. They need to protect their faces from the dry air and **sand**.

4 The Tuareg men have many customs about their face. They start to cover their faces at age twenty-five. They do not cover their faces for friends. They use black or white **cloth**. The cloth is five yards long. They **wrap** the cloth around their face and neck. You see their eyes, but you don't see their nose and mouth.

5 Every Tuareg man wraps his cloth in a unique way. In this way, everyone knows each other. On **special occasions**, they cover their faces with blue cloth. The blue cloth **rubs** on their faces. Then their faces and face hair are blue. The blue cloth is very expensive, so the rich Tuareg have blue faces. Rich women wear a blue shawl around their shoulders and arms. They rub the shawl on their faces. They want blue faces, too!

6 Tuareg men marry women from the same group. They often marry cousins. The Tuareg women have a lot of freedom. They **decide** important things about their lives. The Tuareg women have long hair and are very beautiful.

7 Today, many Tuareg do not live in the desert. Countries around the Sahara Desert do not want groups of people going from place to place. Many Tuareg now live in towns. Soon it will be hard to find the Blue Men of the Sahara.

VOCABULARY

MEANING

Write the correct words in the blanks.

cloth	cover	sand
wrap	decide	rubs

1. The men _____ their faces. They put something over their faces.
2. The Sahara has _____ everywhere. The ground is like powder.
3. The man has a blue piece of material. He puts this _____ on his face.
4. The men _____ the cloth around their faces. You can see their eyes. You can't see their noses and mouths.
5. The women choose what to do about different things. They _____ what to do.
6. The cloth moves and presses on their faces. The cloth _____ on them.

WORDS THAT GO TOGETHER

Write the correct words in the blanks.

made of	special occasions	place to place	put up

1. The women build a place to eat and sleep. They _____ tents.
2. The men don't wear the blue cloth every day. They wear it on _____.
3. Long ago, the Tuareg built tents with animal skins. Today, tents are _____ plastic.
4. First he went to Morocco. Then he went to Algeria. Then he went to Tunisia. He went from _____.

USE

Work with a partner to answer the questions. Use complete sentences.

1. What are your shoes *made of*?
2. What do you wear on *special occasions*?
3. Where do you see *sand*?
4. Where do women *cover* their faces?
5. What things do people *wrap*?
6. What is something you *put up*?

COMPREHENSION

UNDERSTANDING THE READING

Circle the letter of the correct answer.

1. The Tuareg _____.
   a. move from place to place   b. live in the same place   c. live alone

2. The Tuareg men _____.
   a. cover their eyes   b. wear blue every day   c. cover their faces

3. The Tuareg women _____.
   a. live alone   b. have freedom   c. don't want blue faces

REMEMBERING DETAILS

Reread the passage and answer the questions.

1. How many Tuareg are there today?
2. What is a name for the Tuareg people?
3. At what age do men cover their faces?
4. When do the men cover their faces with a blue cloth?
5. Why do the rich have blue faces?
6. Who do the Tuareg often marry?
7. Where do many Tuareg live today?

SENTENCE COMPLETION

Match the words in Column A and Column B to make sentences.

A	B
____ 1. The women put up	a. in towns.
____ 2. The women do not	b. the tents.
____ 3. The Tuareg have	c. cover their faces.
____ 4. The blue cloth rubs	d. the animals.
____ 5. Today the Tuareg live	e. a difficult life.
____ 6. The men take care of	f. on their faces.

DICTATION

Work with a partner. Read three sentences from the exercise above. Your partner listens and writes the sentences. Then your partner reads three sentences and you write them.

DISCUSSION

Discuss the answers to these questions with your classmates.

1. What do you wear on special occasions?
2. Is it good to move from place to place? Why?
3. Would you like to visit the Sahara Desert? Why or why not?

WRITING

Complete the sentences about the Tuareg.

Example: The Tuareg live _in the Sahara Desert._ _____

1. The Tuareg move _____
2. The Tuareg have _____
3. The Tuareg live _____
4. The men _____
5. The women _____

SPELLING AND PUNCTUATION

 CAPITAL LETTERS: GEOGRAPHICAL NAMES

> **We use a capital letter for names of geographical places, like deserts, mountains, lakes, seas, oceans, rivers, and gulfs. We do <u>not</u> use a capital letter for *the* or *of* in the name.**
>
> *They live in the **S**ahara **D**esert.*
>
> **We do <u>not</u> use a capital letter for a place with no special name.**
>
> *They live in the desert.*

A. Underline the words that need capital letters. Remember the capital letter rules from other units.

1. There are no Tuareg in the gobi desert.
2. There are mountains in the sahara.
3. The nile river is in africa.
4. The atlas mountains are on the edge of the sahara desert.
5. The highest mountain in the sahara is mount tahat.
6. mount everest is higher than mount tahat.
7. Some seas have names of colors, like the yellow sea, the black sea, the red sea, and the white sea.
8. The highest mountain in africa is kilimanjaro.
9. The suez canal is between the indian ocean and the mediterranean sea.
10. The biggest lake in africa is lake victoria.

B. Answer the questions. Use correct capital letters.

1. What are the oceans or seas around or near Africa?

   _____

2. What is the largest river in Africa?

   _____

3. What is the highest mountain in Africa?

   _____

UNIT 17

What Is Canada's Favorite Sport?

BEFORE YOU READ

Answer these questions.

1. What are some popular team sports?
2. What sports can you play in snow or ice?
3. Do people around the world like the same sports?

What Is Canada's Favorite Sport?

1 Canada's favorite sport is ice hockey. All over Canada today, men, women, boys, and girls play hockey. Hockey began in Canada. But we do not know exactly how it began.

2 **At first**, hockey did not have rules. Then, in 1880, Canadian students at McGill University in Montreal made the first rules for ice hockey. These rules changed in 1911 and 1912. The new rules had lines on the ice to make special **areas**. There were also six players on a **team**. This is **similar to** hockey today.

3 Ice hockey is the world's fastest game. Players often **skate** thirty miles an hour. They get tired quickly. Often, hockey players leave a game and other players come in. In hockey, players use a stick to hit a puck. A puck is like a ball, but it is **flat**. It **slides** on the ice. It is better to use a cold puck because it slides faster. Players put the puck in the freezer before a game. In some games, players use more than thirty pucks!

4 Hockey looks easy to play, but it isn't easy. Players try to hit the puck into the other team's goal. The puck goes faster than the players. Pucks go about one hundred miles an hour. Hockey is a **dangerous** game. Many players **get hurt**. Today, players wear special clothes to protect their bodies. The player near the goal wears a mask to protect his face. A player with no mask can break his nose or teeth. In the past, there were many players with no front teeth.

5 **Professional** hockey teams in Canada and the United States play in the NHL. This means the National Hockey League. The NHL started in 1917. Today the NHL has thirty teams in North America. Twenty-four of the teams are in the United States, but most of the players are Canadian. In the spring, millions of people watch the **final** hockey game of the year on television. The winner gets the Stanley Cup. The Stanley Cup is the **prize** for the best hockey team.

6 People around the world play hockey now. It is popular in the Olympics. But hockey will always be Canada's special game.

VOCABULARY

MEANING

Write the correct words in the blanks.

slides	areas	dangerous	final	skate
professional	team	prize	flat	

1. Hockey players do not walk on the ice. They wear special shoes to _____ on the ice.

2. The puck moves smoothly on the ice. It _____.

3. People do not play hockey alone. They play hockey on a _____ with other people.

4. There are many hockey games in the year. The last game is called the _____ game.

5. Hockey players sometimes fall and get hit. Hockey is _____.

6. The best hockey team gets the Stanley Cup. This is the greatest _____ in hockey.

7. A hockey puck is _____. It is smooth. It is not like a ball.

8. Players in the NHL get money to play. It is their job to play hockey. They are _____ players.

9. The hockey puck goes to many different places on the ice. It goes to different _____.

WORDS THAT GO TOGETHER

Write the correct words in the blanks.

get hurt	similar to	at first

1. In the beginning, hockey didn't have rules. Today, hockey has rules. _____, hockey was different from hockey today.

2. Ice hockey in 1911 was about the same as hockey today. They are _____ each other.

3. Hockey players sometimes fall and break bones. They _____.

USE

Work with a partner to answer the questions. Use complete sentences.

1. What other sport is *dangerous*?
2. What sports *team* do you like?
3. What is a famous *prize* in sports?
4. What game is football *similar to*?
5. When do you *slide*?
6. What is something that is *flat*?

COMPREHENSION

UNDERSTANDING THE READING

Circle the letter of the correct answer.

1. Ice hockey is _____.
   a. the world's easiest game
   b. the world's fastest game
   c. the world's newest game

2. The NHL _____.
   a. has thirty teams in North America
   b. started in 1911
   c. does not play in the spring

3. Players change during a game because _____.
   a. they get cold
   b. they need a new puck
   c. they get tired

REMEMBERING DETAILS

Reread the passage and answer the questions.

1. Who made the first rules for ice hockey?
2. How many players are on a hockey team?
3. How fast do players go?
4. What do players hit with a stick?
5. Why do players wear special clothes?
6. What is the name of the prize the best hockey team gets?

SENTENCE COMPLETION

Match the words in Column A and Column B to make sentences.

A	B
____ 1. A puck	a. play hockey.
____ 2. Players wear	b. a dangerous game.
____ 3. Canadian students	c. slides on the ice.
____ 4. Hockey began	d. special clothes to protect their bodies.
____ 5. Hockey is	e. made the first rules for hockey.
____ 6. People around the world	f. in Canada.

DICTATION

Work with a partner. Read three sentences from the exercise above. Your partner listens and writes the sentences. Then your partner reads three sentences and you write them.

DISCUSSION

Discuss the answers to these questions with your classmates.

1. What is your favorite team sport?
2. What is the most popular sport in your country?
3. Do you play any sports? Which ones?

WRITING

Complete the sentences about ice hockey.

Example: Ice hockey is _Canada's favorite sport._ _____

1. Ice hockey is _____
2. Players wear_____
3. Players use _____
4. Professional hockey teams _____
5. The Stanley Cup is _____

SPELLING AND PUNCTUATION

APOSTROPHES: POSSESSION

> **We use an apostrophe (') to show possession.**
>
> Singular noun <u>not</u> ending in –s: **'s**   *Canada**'s** favorite sport is ice hockey.*
>
> Singular noun ending in –s: **'** <u>or</u> **'s**   *Chris**'** brother plays for the NHL.*
>
> <u>or</u>
>
> *Chris**'s** brother plays for the NHL.*
>
> Plural noun <u>not</u> ending in –s: **'s**   *The women**'s** games are dangerous, too.*
>
> Plural noun ending in –s: **'**   *The players**'** sticks are new.*

A. Underline the words that need apostrophes to show possession. Write the correct words on the lines.

1. The <u>worlds</u> fastest game is hockey.   *world's*

2. The professional players salaries are high.   _____

3. The childrens favorite sport is hockey.   _____

4. James shot was great.   _____

5. The womens hockey team is good.   _____

6. Next years game is in Montreal.   _____

7. The players skate is broken.   _____

8. The teams Stanley Cup is beautiful.   _____

B. Write two sentences with apostrophes to show possession.

_____

_____

UNIT 18

Where Is the Outback?

Answer these questions.

1. What do you see in the picture?
2. What kind of life do the people have there?
3. Would you like to live there?

Where Is the Outback?

1 About one-half of Australia is desert. This area is the Outback. The name comes from the words "out in the back of the mountains and cities." The weather is very hot and dry, and the winds are **strong**. Sometimes there is no rain for many years. But when it rains, there is water everywhere! Not many people live in the Outback.

2 The people in the Outback have cattle or sheep farms. The farms are called stations. The stations are very big. Some stations are as big as a small country. Life is difficult because everything is **far away**. Sometimes it takes a day or two to drive to the next station. Towns are usually far away, too. People go to town **once** a week or once a month.

3 The station homes are very large because they have many **purposes**. They must be big so visitors can sleep there. Houses also have large rooms to keep **extra** things. Families buy a lot of food and **supplies** in town.

4 Life in the Outback is different in other ways. People get **mail** once a week. Children don't go to school every day. They study with a school called the School of the Air. The teacher and student talk to each other with a special radio. Most stations have an area for airplanes to land. It is like the station's own airport. Sick people call the Royal Flying Doctor service. A doctor **gives advice** over the radio. In an emergency, the doctor **picks up** the sick people in an airplane. Then they go to the nearest hospital.

5 People in the Outback are careful when they travel. Before a farmer travels to town, he tells a friend. The friend knows what time the farmer is coming. If the farmer is **late**, his friend knows there is a problem. The friend will look for the farmer. People must know how to do many things. They must know how to fix their car if it **breaks down**. They always carry extra gasoline, water, and parts for their car.

6 Life in the Outback is very difficult, but it is good, too. Here you are close to nature, and there are many unusual animals. You also have a lot of freedom.

VOCABULARY

MEANING

Write the correct words in the blanks.

once	extra	supplies	purposes
late	mail	strong	

1. The winds have a lot of power and force. The winds are _____.
2. Farmers go to the town one time every week. They go _____ a week.
3. People get letters, cards, and packages at their house. They get _____.
4. The farmer was going to meet his friend at three o'clock. He met him at four o'clock. He was _____.
5. People do many different things at the station house. They sleep there and they keep things there. The house has many _____.
6. People buy _____ in town. They buy different things that they need.
7. The family drinks one bottle of milk every day. They keep two bottles of milk in the house. They keep _____ milk.

WORDS THAT GO TOGETHER

Write the correct words in the blanks.

gives advice	breaks down	far away	picks up

1. Sick people talk to the doctor over the radio. The doctor _____. He tells people what to do.
2. The town is not near the house. It takes a long time to get to the house. The town is _____.
3. His car sometimes _____. It stops working, and then he fixes it.
4. The doctor brings sick people to the hospital. He _____ the people in a truck or an airplane. Then they go to the hospital together.

USE

Work with a partner to answer the questions. Use complete sentences.

1. What *supplies* do you keep in your house?
2. Who gives *advice* to you?
3. What do you do *once* a week?
4. What *mail* do you usually get?
5. What friend lives *far away* from you?

COMPREHENSION

UNDERSTANDING THE READING

Circle the letter of the correct answer.

1. The Outback is _____.
   a. in the back of   b. the desert area of   c. on top of a mountain
      Australia   Australia

2. The people in the Outback live _____.
   a. near water   b. near towns   c. on big farms

3. In the Outback, people _____.
   a. are careful when   b. go to town once   c. fly to school
      they travel   a year

REMEMBERING DETAILS

Circle *T* if the sentence is true. Circle *F* if the sentence is false.

1. It rains all the time in the Outback.   T   F

2. Small towns are called stations.   T   F

3. Children go to school every day.   T   F

4. In the Outback, people buy a lot of food at one time.   T   F

5. People in the Outback always have extra gasoline.   T   F

6. Sick people visit a doctor.   T   F

SENTENCE COMPLETION

Match the words in Column A and Column B to make sentences.

A	B
____ 1. The Outback has	a. very large.
____ 2. Houses have	b. very difficult.
____ 3. Station homes are	c. many unusual animals.
____ 4. Children don't go	d. large storerooms.
____ 5. Families buy	e. to school every day.
____ 6. Life in the Outback is	f. food and supplies.

DICTATION

Work with a partner. Read three sentences from the exercise above. Your partner listens and writes the sentences. Then your partner reads three sentences and you write them.

DISCUSSION

Discuss the answers to these questions with your classmates.

1. Would you like to live in the Outback? Why or why not?
2. People in the Outback keep a lot of supplies. What supplies are important? Why?
3. Is it better to go to a school or study at home? Explain.

WRITING

Complete the sentences about the Outback.

Example: The Outback is _in Australia._

1. The weather in the Outback _____
2. The people in the Outback _____
3. The station homes _____
4. Children in the Outback _____
5. Life in the Outback _____

SPELLING AND PUNCTUATION

 CAPITAL LETTERS: SCHOOLS, COLLEGES, AND COURSES

We use a capital letter for the name of a school, college, university, or course. We do not use a capital letter for *of* or *the* in the name.

*In the Outback, children study with the **S**chool of the **A**ir.*

*I'm taking **H**istory 33.* (name of course)

We do not use a capital letter for a school subject with no special course name.

I love history. (subject)

A. Underline the words that need capital letters. Remember the capital letter rules from other units.

1. Children can study mathematics.
2. I am taking math 101.
3. I heard claremont college is a good college.
4. My friends are going to the university of melbourne.
5. I'm going to study english at language links college in australia.
6. About 140 children in the Outback go to the alice springs school of the air.
7. Next semester, I'm taking biology 220.
8. I want to study business.

B. Answer the questions. Use correct capital letters.

1. What is the name of your school? _____
2. What is the name of the course you are taking? _____
3. What school subjects do you want to take? _____

UNIT 19

Why Is the Elephant Important in Thailand?

BEFORE YOU READ

Answer these questions.

1. What do you know about elephants?
2. Where do you see elephants?
3. What do elephants do?

Why Is the Elephant Important in Thailand?

1 Elephants are a very important part of Thailand's history. They are symbols of **power** and peace. They are strong and **gentle** at the same time. But many years ago, they also did important work. They helped the Thai people get wood from their forests.

2 In the past, the Thai people **cut down** a lot of trees. In 1989, the government made a law to stop this. They wanted to keep the trees in the forest. Today, the Thai people cut down only a few trees. Some elephants work in the forests to help them. The forests are in the mountains. Many trucks and machines cannot go up the mountains. But elephants can. Men cut down the trees, and the elephants pick up the trees. Then the elephants **carry** the trees to the river. The trees **float** down the river to other men. The men cut the trees into pieces of wood.

3 In the past, elephants **trained** for many years to learn how to work. Each elephant had its own trainer, or *mahout*. A *mahout* **spent his life** with the same elephant. Fathers wanted their sons to be *mahouts,* too. *Mahouts* bought baby elephants for their sons. First, the baby elephant stayed with its mother. When the elephant was three years old, it lived with the boy. The boy and the elephant grew up together. The boy took care of the elephant. They learned a lot about each other.

4 A *mahout* trained, fed, and took care of his elephant. This was a difficult job. An elephant eats 550 pounds (250 kilos) of plants and drinks 80 gallons (300 liters) of water every day! It trained every day for six hours in the morning. The elephant **got used to** the *mahout*. The elephant remembered the *mahout's* **voice** and smell. It understood its *mahout's* **instructions**. The elephant obeyed its *mahout*. It did not obey other *mahouts*. The *mahout* trained the elephant for twenty years. At age twenty, the elephant began to work. Elephants worked for about thirty-five years. They stopped work at age fifty-five or sixty—like people.

5 Today, most elephants and *mahouts* have no work. But the elephants are still very important in Thailand. Visitors to Thailand want to see them. The Thai people are very **proud of** their elephants.

VOCABULARY

MEANING

Write the correct words in the blanks.

| instructions | voice | carry | power |
| trained | float | gentle | |

1. The elephant is a _____ animal. It is very nice. It doesn't hurt people.

2. The trees lay in the water. They stay on top of the water. The trees _____.

3. The elephants hold the trees and take them to another place. They _____ the trees.

4. In Thailand, people _____ elephants. They taught them to do work.

5. The elephant is a symbol of _____. It is very big and strong.

6. The *mahout* speaks in a certain way. The elephant knows how the *mahout* sounds. The elephant knows its *mahout's* _____.

7. The *mahout* says to do something. Then the elephant does it. The elephant listens to the *mahout's* _____.

WORDS THAT GO TOGETHER

Write the correct words in the blanks.

| got used to | proud of | cut down | spent his life |

1. The *mahout* was with the elephant every day. He _____ with the elephant.

2. The Thai people are happy about their elephants. They think the elephants are good. The Thai people are _____ them.

3. The men want the tree to fall to the ground. They use a big knife or a machine. The men _____ the tree.

4. The *mahouts* and the elephants knew each other very well. They were good friends. They _____ each other.

USE

Work with a partner to answer the questions. Use complete sentences.

1. Who are you *proud of*?
2. What animal do people *train*?
3. What animal has a lot of *power*?
4. What animal is *gentle*?
5. When do you follows *instructions* in class?
6. Which singer has a good *voice*?

COMPREHENSION

UNDERSTANDING THE READING

Circle the letter of the correct answer.

1. Elephants in Thailand are symbols of _____.
   a. trees and forests   b. power and peace   c. work and play

2. Elephants work in the _____.
   a. forests   b. trucks   c. rivers

3. Elephants can _____.
   a. float down the river   b. cut down trees   c. go up mountains

REMEMBERING DETAILS

Circle *T* if the sentence is true. Circle *F* if the sentence is false.

1.	Elephants did important work in Thailand.	T	F
2.	The men carry the trees to the river.	T	F
3.	The elephants trained every day for three hours.	T	F
4.	The elephant begins to work at age thirty-five.	T	F
5.	A *mahout* trained, fed, and took care of his elephant.	T	F
6.	Today elephants have no work.	T	F

SENTENCE COMPLETION

Match the words in Column A and Column B to make sentences.

A	B
____ 1. An elephant understood	a. in the forests.
____ 2. The elephant worked	b. strong and gentle.
____ 3. The elephant is	c. and took care of his elephant.
____ 4. A *mahout* trained	d. its *mahout's* instructions.
____ 5. Elephants trained	e. trees to the river.
____ 6. Elephants carry	f. for twenty years.

DICTATION

Work with a partner. Read three sentences from the exercise above. Your partner listens and writes the sentences. Then your partner reads three sentences and you write them.

DISCUSSION

Discuss the answers to these questions with your classmates.

1. Some people think it is bad to make animals work. What do you think?
2. What is your favorite animal? Why?
3. Elephants are intelligent. What other animals are intelligent? How do they help people?

WRITING

Complete the sentences about elephants.

Example: Elephants are *a very important part of Thailand's history.*

1. Elephants helped _____
2. Elephants worked _____
3. Elephants trained _____
4. The *mahout* _____
5. Today, most elephants _____

SPELLING AND PUNCTUATION

WORDS WITH *PH* THAT SOUNDS LIKE *F*

In some words, we spell the *f* sound with *ph*.

*ph*ysics   ele*ph*ant   paragra*ph*

A. Circle the correctly spelled word in each group. You may use a dictionary.

1. pharmacy   farmacy   parmacy   3. nefew   nephew   nefhew

2. frase   phrase   pfrase   4. hyphen   hyfen   hypen

B. Underline the misspelled words. Write the correct sentences on the lines.

1. Elefants work in the phorests of Thailand.

   _____

2. I am reading about the geografy of Thailand.

   _____

3. Thailand's shape is like an elefant's head. It's phunny!

   _____

4. Here's a fhoto of my nefew on an elefant.

   _____

5. I will fone my Thai friend to ask about elefants.

   _____

6. This elepant is an orfan. He has no mother or phather.

   _____

7. This biografy is about the liphe of a *mahout*. It's phantastic!

   _____

8. My phriend is going from Filadelfia to Thailand.

   _____

UNIT 20

How Did Rich Romans Live?

BEFORE YOU READ

Answer these questions.

1. Who are the people in the picture?
2. Where and when did they live?
3. Do you think they are rich or poor? Why?

How Did Rich Romans Live?

1 Over 2,000 years ago, there were many rich people in Rome. The Roman government controlled a lot of land. They controlled most of Europe. The Romans **forced** everyone to use Roman customs. Everyone paid Roman taxes and **obeyed** Roman laws. The government workers had to speak Latin. Latin was the language of Rome.

2 Rich Romans had two houses. They had one house in **the country** and one house in the city. The houses had many rooms. There was a garden in the middle. The floors and walls had beautiful tiles. Artists painted pictures on the tiles. The houses had water, a kitchen, and heating. Most people at that time didn't have these things. Many rich Romans had slaves. The slaves cooked and cleaned. Romans took men, women, and children from other countries to work as slaves.

3 The Romans ate three meals a day. They ate the main meal in the afternoon. They ate for **several** hours. Rich families asked friends to **come over** for a big meal. They had special foods, like mice, oysters, and peacock. They ate with their fingers or a spoon. During meals, Romans didn't sit on chairs. They lay on **sofas**!

4 Most Romans went to **public** baths. They **relaxed** and met friends there. They swam in the pools, read, ate, and **got a haircut**. There were three kinds of baths: very cold, warm, and hot. Romans cleaned their bodies in another way. They rubbed olive oil on their bodies. Then they took it off with a knife. They believed clean people were very **healthy**.

5 Rich Romans were always clean. The men shaved their face hair and had short haircuts. Some men **dyed** their hair black. Women had long hair and wore makeup. They put powder on their faces and put color on their lips. The Romans also wanted to smell clean. They used a lot of perfume. They used different perfumes for different parts of their bodies. They put perfume on their furniture, clothes, and horses, too.

6 The rich Romans had interesting lives. Today we use many things from the Romans, such as perfume, glass windows, and even ketchup!

VOCABULARY

MEANING

Write the correct words in the blanks.

forced	several	obeyed	public
healthy	sofas	relaxed	dyed

1. People did not like Roman customs. But the Romans wanted everyone to use their customs. The Romans _____ people to use their customs.

2. They ate meals for more than two or three hours. They ate for _____ hours.

3. Everyone in town went to the baths. The baths were _____.

4. The Romans were happy at the baths. They didn't worry about their problems. They _____.

5. The people did what the Romans told them to do. The people _____ the Romans.

6. The men added color to their hair. They _____ their hair.

7. They lay on long seats called _____.

8. Romans did not want to be sick. They wanted to be _____.

WORDS THAT GO TOGETHER

Write the correct words in the blanks.

got a haircut	the country	come over

1. The Romans wanted their friends to visit their houses. They wanted their friends to _____.

2. The Romans had houses outside of the city. They had houses in _____.

3. The Romans wanted to look good. Sometimes the hair on their head was too long. Then they _____.

USE

Work with a partner to answer the questions. Use complete sentences.

1. When do you get a *haircut*?
2. Where do you see *sofas*?
3. What do you do to be *healthy*?
4. What do you see in *the country*?
5. What do you do to *relax*?
6. When do your friends *come over*?

COMPREHENSION

UNDERSTANDING THE READING

Circle the letter of the correct answer.

1. Rich Romans wanted everyone to _____.
   a. go to Europe   b. live in the city   c. use Roman customs

2. The Romans ate _____.
   a. several meals a day   b. the main meal in the afternoon   c. three main meals

3. The Romans went to the public baths to _____.
   a. get clean   b. use perfume   c. lay on sofas

REMEMBERING DETAILS

Reread the passage and answer the questions.

1. What did the Roman government control?
2. What did the Romans' houses have?
3. What did the Romans eat with?
4. What did the Romans do at the public baths?
5. What color did the men dye their hair?
6. What did they put perfume on?

SENTENCE COMPLETION

Match the words in Column A and Column B to make sentences.

A	B
____ 1. The houses had	a. for several hours.
____ 2. The Romans ate	b. to the public baths.
____ 3. Romans were	c. many rooms.
____ 4. Romans went	d. always clean.
____ 5. The Romans used	e. to obey their laws.
____ 6. The Romans forced people	f. different perfumes.

DICTATION

Work with a partner. Read three sentences from the exercise above. Your partner listens and writes the sentences. Then your partner reads three sentences and you write them.

DISCUSSION

Discuss the answers to these questions with your classmates.

1. Would you like to live like a rich Roman? Why or why not?
2. Rich Romans had a house in the city and a house in the country. Which kind of house is better? Why?
3. Do you like to invite friends to come over? What do you like to do with them?

WRITING

Complete the sentences about the rich Romans.

Example: The Roman government controlled <u>a lot of land.</u>

1. The Romans wanted _____
2. The houses had _____
3. The Romans ate _____
4. The Romans went _____
5. The Romans liked to be _____

SPELLING AND PUNCTUATION

 IRREGULAR PLURALS

Some singular nouns end in –f or –fe. For –f, we change the –f to –v and add –es.

self—sel**ves**   half—hal**ves**

For –fe, we change the –f to –v and add –s after the –e.

life—li**ves**   wife—wi**ves**

Some words have special rules.

roof—roo**fs**   chief—chie**fs**

belief—belie**fs**   chef—che**fs**

Some words do not use –s for the plural. They have a special spelling.

man—men   woman—women   child—children

foot—feet   tooth—teeth   mouse—mice

A. Circle the correctly spelled word in each group. You may use a dictionary.

1. loafs   loaves   loafes

2. halfs   halvs   halves

3. chiefs   chieves   chievs

4. scarvs   scarfs   scarves

5. rooves   roofs   roovs

6. thieves   thiefs   thiefes

7. leafes   leaves   leafs

8. shelves   shelfs   shelfes

B. Underline the incorrect plurals. Write the correct plurals on the lines.

1. The mans had short hair.   _____

2. The womens wore makeup.   _____

3. They used knifes to clean their bodies.   _____

4. A rich Roman did not have many wifes.   _____

5. Rich Romans had good lifes.   _____

6. They took care of themselfes.   _____

7. They liked to eat mouses.   _____

SELF-TEST 2

Units 11–20

A. SENTENCE COMPLETION

Circle the letter of the correct answer.

1. Andrew Carnegie _____.
   a. be from a poor family
   b. was from a poor family
   c. was from a family poor
   d. being from a poor family

2. _____ everywhere.
   a. There has huge glaciers
   b. There have huge glaciers
   c. There are glaciers huge
   d. There are huge glaciers

3. Miners _____ in Coober Pedy in 1915.
   a. discovering opals
   b. discovers opals
   c. they discovered opals
   d. discovered opals

4. Some people _____ to fix and clean their teeth.
   a. spend a lot of money
   b. to be spending a lot of money
   c. spends a lot of money
   d. to spend a lot of money

5. In 1859, Henry Dunant _____.
   a. go to Italy
   b. to Italy went
   c. went to Italy
   d. go Italy

6. The Tuareg _____ their faces for friends.
   a. do not covers
   b. do not cover
   c. not cover
   d. not do covers

7. Hockey _____.
   a. began in Canada
   b. in Canada began
   c. begin in Canada
   d. to begin in Canada

8. About one-half of Australia _____.
   a. have desert   c. be desert
   b. desert has   d. is desert

9. _____ in Thailand.
   a. Elephants is very important   c. Elephants be very important
   b. Elephants are very important   d. Elephants very important

10. The Romans _____ clean.
    a. was always   c. were always
    b. be always   d. always was

B. VOCABULARY

Complete the definitions. Circle the letter of the correct answer.

1. You do something immediately. You do it _____.
   a. as much as possible   b. right away   c. by now   d. nearly

2. Something very, very big is _____.
   a. dangerous   b. normal   c. attractive   d. huge

3. You want to make a hole in the ground. You _____ in the ground.
   a. cover   b. drop   c. dig   d. decide

4. You pull something to make it bigger. You _____ it.
   a. stretch   b. spread   c. return   d. train

5. People are hurt in a fight or war. They are _____.
   a. dangerous   b. wrapped   c. wounded   d. discovered

6. You put one thing on top of another. People can't see it. You _____ it.
   a. drop   b. dig   c. rub   d. cover

7. One thing is like another thing. It is _____ it.
   a. similar to   b. made of   c. side by side   d. belongs to

8. You have the things you need. Then you get more things. You get
   _____ things.
   a. extra   b. late   c. normal   d. main

9. You follow rules or orders. You follow _____.
   a. teams   b. instructions   c. purposes   d. supplies

10. You tell people to do something and they do it. They _____ you.
    a. decide   b. entertain   c. relax   d. obey

C. SPELLING AND PUNCTUATION

Circle the letter of the sentence with the correct spelling and punctuation.

1. a. Andrew Carnegie gave away over $350 millions.
   b. Andrew Carnegie gave away over $350s million.
   c. Andrew Carnegie gave away over $350 million.
   d. Andrew Carnegie gave away over $350 Million.

2. a. Ships go to Antarctica during the Summer months from November to February.
   b. Ships go to antarctica during the summer months from november to february.
   c. Ships go to Antarctica during the summer months from November to February.
   d. Ships go to Antarctica during the summer months from November to february.

3. a. Coober Pedy is in Australia!
   b. Thousands of people live underground!
   c. Where is Australia!
   d. The native people are called Aborigines!

4. a. People get tattooss to show they belong to a group.
   b. People get tattoos to show they belong to a group.
   c. People get tattooes to show they belong to a group.
   d. People get Tattoos to show they belong to a group.

5. a. The Red Cross is the Red Crescent in muslim countries.
   b. The red cross is the red crescent in Muslim countries.
   c. The Red Cross is the Red Crescent in Muslim countries.
   d. The Red cross is the Red crescent in Muslim countries.

6. a. The Tuareg live in the Sahara Desert in Africa.
   b. The Tuareg live in the sahara desert in Africa.
   c. The Tuareg live in The Sahara Desert in Africa.
   d. The Tuareg live in the Sahara desert in Africa.

7. a. Canadas favorite sport is hockey.
   b. Canadas' favorite sport is hockey.
   c. Canada favorite sport is hockey.
   d. Canada's favorite sport is hockey.

8. a. Children in the Outback study with the school of the air.
   b. Children in the Outback study with the School of the Air.
   c. Children in the Outback study with The School of the Air.
   d. Children in the Outback study with The School Of The Air.

9. a. This biography about a *mahout* is phantastic!
   b. This biografhy about a *mahout* is fantastic!
   c. This biografy about a *mahout* is fantastic!
   d. This biography about a *mahout* is fantastic!

10. a. The rich Romans had interesting live.
    b. The rich Romans had interesting lives.
    c. The rich Romans had interesting life.
    d. The rich Romans had interesting lifes.

APPENDICES

WORD LIST

UNIT 1

Vocabulary Words

adults	interview
alone	quiet
author	special

Words that Go Together

all over the world	make money
came true	took care of
free time	

UNIT 2

Vocabulary Words

act	practice
bright	superstitions
calendar	sweep
celebration	traditions
culture	

Words that Go Together

good luck
look like
put away

UNIT 3

Vocabulary Words

bowls	garden
emergency	politicians
flag	prepares
floor	

Words that Go Together

a lot of
follow rules
on top of
the rest of

UNIT 4

Vocabulary Words

cost	problem
decorate	repairs
farms	simple
ground	soft
hit	

Words that Go Together

against the law
for a long time
spends money on

UNIT 5

Vocabulary Words

bones	midnight
candles	remember
favorite	skeleton
meal	towel

Words that Go Together

get together
have a picnic
tell stories

UNIT 6

Vocabulary Words

chewed	raw
control	shared
custom	skins
hard	wood
pulled	

Words that Go Together

at the same time
each other
from time to time
keep in touch with

UNIT 7

Vocabulary Words

concerts	hit	
copied	joined	
fans	screamed	
group	together	

Words that Go Together

broke up
in all
in the world
taught themselves

UNIT 8

Vocabulary Words

added	modern
along	protect
buried	space
exactly	structure

Words that Go Together

care about
comes from
fell down
grew up

UNIT 9

Vocabulary Words

afford	foreigner
agree	groom
bride	reasons
couple	salary
expensive	

Words that Go Together

asks for
brand name
the same as

UNIT 10

Vocabulary Words

cartoons	immediate
exciting	polite
guests	signs
ideas	

Words that Go Together

amusement park	looked around
famous for	made sure
have fun	

UNIT 11

Vocabulary Words

bridges	peace
factory	realized
let	saved
nearly	throughout

Words that Go Together

as much as possible
give away
named after
right away

UNIT 12

Vocabulary Words

blows	huge
continent	separate
dropped	temperature
empty	unique
experiment	

Words that Go Together

belong to
had no choice
in all

UNIT 13

Vocabulary Words

deep	main
dig	native
discovered	view
holes	

Words that Go Together

in the future
look for
of course

UNIT 14

Vocabulary Words

attractive	spread	
lips	straight	
normal	stretches	
returned		

Words that Go Together

belong to	stick out
pull out	take off
puts in	

UNIT 15

Vocabulary Words

journalist	signed
resigned	symbol
reverse	volunteers
shocked	wounded

Words that Go Together

by now
lost money
on business

UNIT 16

Vocabulary Words

cloth	rubs
cover	sand
decide	wrap

Words that Go Together

made of
place to place
put up
special occasions

UNIT 17

Vocabulary Words

areas	professional
dangerous	skate
final	slides
flat	team
prize	

Words that Go Together

at first
get hurt
similar to

UNIT 18

Vocabulary Words

extra	purposes
late	strong
mail	supplies
once	

Words that Go Together

breaks down
far away
gives advice
picks up

UNIT 19

Vocabulary Words

carry	power
float	trained
gentle	voice
instructions	

Words that Go Together

cut down
got used to
side by side
spent his life

UNIT 20

Vocabulary Words

dyed	public
forced	relaxed
healthy	several
obeyed	sofas

Words that Go Together

come over
got a haircut
the country

MAP OF THE WORLD

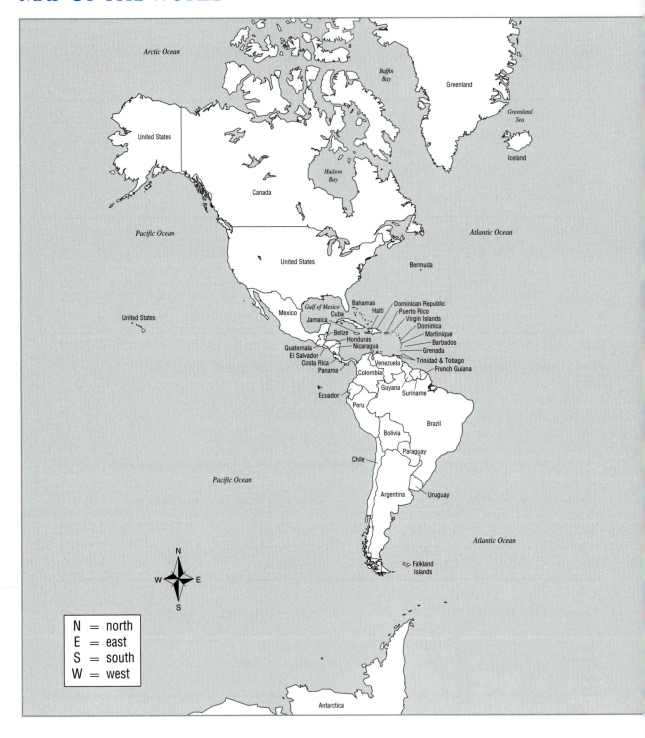

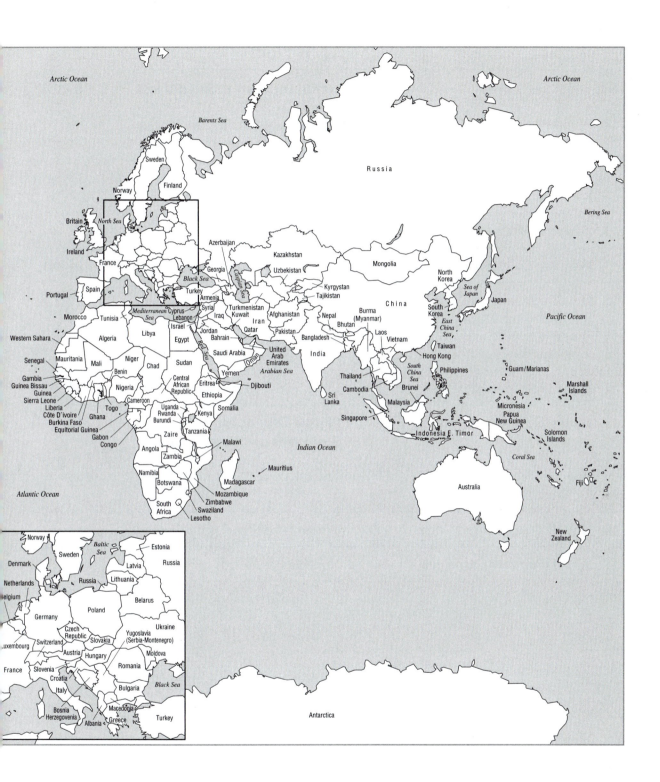

INDEX TO THE SPELLING AND PUNCTUATION ACTIVITIES